MW00789760

Inflation: A Management Guide To Company Survival

INFLATION: A Management Guide to Company Survival

Edited by Christopher J. West

A HALSTED PRESS BOOK

JOHN WILEY & SONS
New York – Toronto

English language edition, except USA and Canada published by
Associated Business Programmes Ltd
17 Buckingham Gate, London SW1

Published in USA and Canada by
Halsted Press, a division of
John Wiley & Sons Inc
New York

First published 1976

Library of Congress catalog number 76–12133

ISBN 0–470–15087–4

Printed in Great Britain by The Anchor Press Ltd
Tiptree, Colchester, Essex

Contents

Introduction

Inflation is far from being a new phenomenon, but until recently modern businesses have been shielded from its worst effects. The rapid rates of inflation which broke upon an unsuspecting world in 1973 were beyond the experience of most companies. Those companies that had learned to live with the great inflation in Germany in the 1930s, and more recently companies operating in Brazil and other Latin American countries, appear to have done little to pass on their experience, perhaps because the environments were so special that few lessons could be drawn that are of immediate relevance to the crises being faced by Western firms today. Sustained rates of inflation in excess of 20 per cent per annum experienced on an international scale is, in any event, itself a new phenomenon.

Of course, the theory of inflation and its probable effects on businesses forms a standard component of economics and business courses throughout the world, but actual experience of how to cope has been very thin on the ground. In a matter of months, therefore, all businesses had to cope with a radically changed business environment. Many have failed to do so successfully and the result has been an alarming increase in the level of bankruptcies. Some companies have been lucky or have had sufficient reserves to ride out the storm. Others have been clever or have retained good advice and, as a result, survived.

Survival has replaced growth as the principal objective in the corporate strategies of all but the most ambitious companies, and in order to survive companies have been forced to take a fresh look at every aspect of their operations. Product and service strategies, production methods, personnel policies, marketing, accounting and finance have all had to respond to rapidly inflating costs and changes in differentials, sometimes painfully. Management has had to take a radically fresh look at its decisions, for what was once the correct response to a problem may have been invalidated by a fundamental shift in costs and operating conditions. Inflation has induced the birth of a range of new techniques, such as inflation accounting, which require evaluation and assimilation.

In all countries the learning process is far from complete and, although abating, inflation is likely to continue at frightening levels for some years to come. Even in those areas that appear to have successfully controlled their inflation rates, there is a prevailing fear that a new bout could all too easily be triggered off again. It therefore seemed appropriate at this time to draw together the major lessons that have been learned or considered in order to provide guidelines for corporate survival in the coming years. The task was daunting because inflation touches on every corner of corporate activity and few single authors could hope to have sufficient specialist experience to treat all the problems adequately. The answer has been to produce an edited book in which specialists write on their own subjects. The subject matter of the book covers all the major corporate activities which are affected by inflationary pressures, including labour, material purchases, investment decisions, accounting, pricing and marketing. We have also included a detailed discussion of indexation, a technique that comes into its own when costs rise rapidly, and to preface the more specific discussions there is a general chapter which provides a natural history of inflation itself. All the chapters are short and to the point and, while avoiding oversimplifications, the authors have attempted to keep their treatment of the subject matter to a level suitable for general management rather than the academic stratosphere.

In a book of this nature the editor is more than normally dependent on his contributors, and I am honoured to have worked with such a distinguished group. Beyond setting the subject matter, excising the purpler prose and standardising the footnotes there is little that I have felt able to attempt. It is for the reader to judge the originality and usefulness of the contributions. As editor, I am grateful for the speed, thoroughness and enthusiasm with which the contributors have approached their tasks. Thanks are also due to the staff of Associated Business Programmes who undertook the organisation and paperwork associated with the book.

Chipstead, Surrey
December 1975

The Contributors: Biographical Notes

CHRISTOPHER J. WEST, B.Sc. Econ., the editor of this book, is a graduate of the London School of Economics. Prior to joining the Board of Industrial Market Research Ltd., where he is now Deputy Managing Director, Mr West worked in the Supply and Planning department of Shell International and as an economist with Eurofinance, a Paris based financial and economic consultancy. He has acquired a broad range of industry and marketing experience and writes frequently on marketing subjects. He is the editor of *Marketing on a Small Budget*.

SAMUEL BRITTAN was educated at Kilburn Grammar School and Jesus College, Cambridge, where he took first-class honours in economics. He then held various posts on the *Financial Times* (1955–61), was Economics Editor of the *Observer* (1961–4), an Adviser at the Department of Economic Affairs (1965), and has been principal economic commentator on the *Financial Times* since 1966. He was the first winner of the Senior Wincott Award for financial journalists in 1971. He was a Research Fellow of Nuffield College in 1973–4 and in 1974 was elected a Visiting Fellow of that College. He is the author of a number of books on economic subjects and his most recent publications include *Capitalism and the Permissive Society, Is there an Economic Consensus?*, and *Second Thoughts on Full Employment Policy*.

JOHN E. BROYLES, B.Sc. (MIT), M.Sc. (RPI), Ph.D (London), is Lecturer in Finance at the London Graduate School of Business Studies where he is Director of the Corporate Finance Programme, a course of study designed for senior financial executives. He attained his doctorate at the London School of Economics where he wrote a thesis on supply and demand on the Stock Exchange. He has extensive industrial experience and was formerly Planning Manager, Ludlow Corporation. His research and publications concern capital markets, institutional investment policy, capital budgeting, corporate financial planning and acquisitions. He is a consultant to a number of multinational companies and to HM Treasury.

DAVID FARMER, M.Sc. Ph.D, is a senior faculty member at The Administrative Staff College, Henley and Brunel University. He has been involved in consultancy and training assignments in the procurement area since 1965 in a wide variety of industries and in most European countries as well as the United States. Prior to 1965 he had thirteen years' experience in procurement and marketing in four industries. He is co-author of five texts and more than one hundred papers, cases and simulation exercises. His doctoral dissertation concerned with procurement and corporate planning in UK-based multinational manufacturing companies was the first in this area of management study.

JULIAN R. FRANKS, B.A. (Sheffield), M.B.A. (Columbia), is Senior Lecturer in Finance at the London Graduate School of Business Studies where he is Director of the Financial Planning and Measurement Programme attended by senior financial and non-financial executives. He received the Masters Degree in Business Administration from Columbia University before joining Standard Oil of New Jersey as an auditor. He then became Senior Auditor in Esso Europe before joining the London Business School. He is the co-author of a book on corporate financial management, and his research and other publications are concerned with the success and failure of mergers in the United Kingdom, corporate finance and inflation. Julian Franks is an active consultant in both the private and public sectors, including HM Treasury.

ROBBIE H. GILBERT was born in 1951 and educated at Paisley Grammar School, Renfrewshire, Scotland, and the University of Lancaster. He took his BA with joint honours in Politics and Philosophy. He then studied law for a year at the Inns of Court.

In February 1973 he joined the Social Affairs Research Department of the Confederation of British Industry. In this capacity he was involved in the study and development of policy on the pay side of the Counter-Inflation policy and the Social Contract. He was also involved on work on employee participation, job satisfaction and related subjects in the employment field, and represented the British employers at various international conferences. In August 1975 he moved to the Conservative Research Department and is currently supervising policy development on employment matters for the Rt. Hon. James Prior, MP, Shadow Secretary of State for Employment.

PATRICK KIRKMAN is a Certified Accountant and Chartered Secretary, and has had extensive experience in commerce, industry and education. He is at present Senior Lecturer in Accountancy Studies at the University of Exeter. He has written extensively on the subject of inflation accounting, and he is the author of two books on the subject—*Accounting under Inflationary Conditions* and *Inflation Accounting—A guide for non-accountants*. Mr Kirkman has very close links with accountants in the business sector, and has led numerous seminars for businessmen on the subject of inflation accounting.

PETER LILLEY is an investment analyst with a prominent City firm. He was previously an economic consultant working mainly in underdeveloped countries. He was National Chairman of the Bow Group, the independent Conservative research organisation, between 1973 and 1975 and stood as Conservative Parliamentary Candidate for Tottenham in 1974.

He has published sundry economic and political pamphlets—notably *Curing Inflation, The Alternative Manifesto* and *Ulster—Do You Sincerely Want to Win?*—and is currently writing a book on Incomes Policy jointly with Samuel Brittan.

A. R. PREST has been Professor of Economics, with special reference to the public sector, at the London School of Economics since 1970. Before that he held appointments in Cambridge and Manchester; he has also been a visiting Professor at various Universities in other countries. He is the author of *Public Finance in Theory and Practice, Public Finance in Developing Countries* and joint editor of *The UK Economy*, as well as of other books and papers in professional journals.

E. J. ROBERTSON, M.A., is Director (Industrial Relations) of the Confederation of British Industry. His previous appointments include Director of Research at the Engineering Employers Feder ation and Central Personnel Executive for the Avon Rubber Company. He has also been a lecturer in the Department of Sociology at the University of Strathclyde. He is a member of a number of Committees dealing with prices and working conditions and his publications include *Local Labour Markets and Wage Payment Systems* and *An Employers Guide to the Employment Protection Act.*

RICHARD SKINNER, B.A., acquired his marketing experience in the office equipment and communications industries. He joined Reliance Systems Limited, a subsidiary of the General Electric

Company, as Sales Manager in 1964. His work since then has included the planning and implementation of a major diversification programme. In 1971 he was appointed marketing director. Published works include *Launching New Products in Competitive Markets,* 'Organising for Marketing on a Small Budget' in *Marketing on a Small Budget*, and *How British Industry Prices* (co-author with Bryan Atkin).

CHAPTER 1

Effects of Inflation on Business Activity

A. R. PREST

The aim in this chapter is to outline a general background as a preparation for the more detailed studies in ensuing chapters. To this end we shall start with a brief factual survey of the course of inflation in recent years; we shall then turn to different explanations of the mechanics of inflation; finally, the third section will discuss the effects of inflation on business profitability and the most appropriate reactions to it.

RECENT INFLATION EXPERIENCE

The indicators of inflation that are most commonly considered relate to prices and earnings movements. If we look at United Kingdom data we find the following pattern:

Table 1.1 UK Retail Prices and Average Weekly Earnings (1970 = 100)

	Retail prices	*Average weekly earnings (all industries)*
1958	66·1	47·7
1959	66·5	49·9
1960	67·2	53·2
1961	69·5	56·4
1962	72·4	58·5
1963	73·8	60·8
1964	76·7	65·1
1965	80·2	70·0
1966	83·2	74·5
1967	85·2	77·0
1968	89·3	83·2
1969	93·9	89·7
1970	100·0	100·0
1971	109·5	111·2
1972	117·0	125·1
1973	126·8	142·4
1974	147·0	(167·5)

Sources: National Institute Economic Review (various issues) and A. R. Prest and D. J. Coppock (eds.), *The UK Economy*, 5th edition, Weidenfeld and Nicholson (London, 1974).

Several points stand out in this tabulation. The first is that, as might be expected, average weekly earnings have risen at a faster rate than prices throughout this period; this simply reflects the annual growth of productivity, sometimes more in one year than another, but nearly always permitting some increase in real earnings. Secondly, there has been a marked tendency for the rate of growth of both prices and earnings to increase over time. Whereas, for instance, prices rose at a rate of something like 3 per cent per annum up to the mid-1960s, there was then a jump, so that the average from 1965–70 was about 4½ per cent. But since 1970 the position has worsened considerably. As Table 1.1 shows, price rises were of the order of 8–10 per cent per annum from 1970–73, but there was then a sharp escalation, with the average level being some 16 per cent higher in 1974 than in 1973. Nor does this tell us the whole story. If one examines the *monthly* prices data one finds that by the winter months of 1974–5 the pattern was that prices were some 20 per cent higher in any given month than in the corresponding month of the preceding winter; in other words, prices were rising at a faster rate at the end of 1974 than earlier in that year. Although the pattern of earnings changes was not identical with that of price changes one can observe the same general tendencies, i.e. a faster rate of growth after 1970 than in previous years and an acceleration by the end of 1974, when earnings were nearly 30 per cent greater than a year earlier.

Attention must now be drawn to another major difference between recent and earlier years. It used to be argued that relatively small variations in the pressure of demand would be sufficient to moderate the rate of inflation; indeed, it was often maintained in the 1960s that reasonable

Table 1.2 UK Manufacturing Gross Trading Profits as a Percentage of Profits plus Employment Income

	1950–71 average	*1972*	*1973*	*1974 1st quarter*	*1974 2nd quarter*
Before Tax	32·0	26·9	29·5	32·8	29·6
Post tax, net of depreciation	20·5	17·1	20·6	23·5	20·5
Post tax, net of depreciation and stock appreciation (RC)[1]	18·3[3]	12·5	12·5	−0·3	2·1
Post tax, net of depreciation and stock appreciation (CPP)[2]	—	13·1	16·5	12·6	6·2

Source: National Institute Economic Review, November 1974, p. 22.

Notes: 1. RC= replacement cost adjustment.
2. CPP= constant purchasing power adjustment.
3. 18·3 figure relates to 1956–71 only.

stability of prices could be attained if only the unemployment rate in Great Britain were allowed to rise from the 1½ per cent or so prevalent in the middle of that decade to 2½ per cent or thereabouts. There was, in fact, much heated controversy on the appropriate rate of unemployment within these limits. But since then unemployment has risen to higher levels (e.g. 3·8 per cent in 1972), whilst price inflation has been markedly worse. In other words, we now have the phenomenon of 'stagflation' where recession and inflation are combined in proportions not previously experienced or contemplated. There are various explanations of this development, but all we need to do at the moment is to note it.

Overall price and earnings indices give us a general view of the inflationary picture, but they conceal many variations in the component parts. Thus, whereas the average annual price rise between 1970 and 1973 was 8·6 per cent, prices of consumer goods and services rose by less (7·8 per cent) but those of investment goods by more (10·7 per cent).[1] There were also variations on the incomes side with, for example, industrial earnings rising faster than salary earnings over the same period. For individual industries and individual businessmen it is clearly insufficient to know only the overall figures when there are pronounced variations between the component parts.

Another set of figures of immense importance to the business world is the movement of profits in recent years. The causal links between inflation and profits are complex, and so one cannot readily attribute changes in one to changes in the other. Nevertheless it is of great importance for our purposes here to note that there has been a marked erosion of profits in recent years. This can be documented from a number of sources,[2] but a simple summary is given in Table 1.2.

Throughout the period 1950–73 there was, in fact, a tendency for the share of profits before tax to fall. Since the mid-1960s there has been a tendency for post-tax profit shares to fall—especially in view of the taxation of stock appreciation in recent years—to such an extent that on a replacement cost basis the post-tax profits share was barely positive in the first half of 1974.[3] We shall have more to say on this subject later.

It should not be thought that the UK experience with inflation is unique. Taking the worst period, i.e. that since 1970, we find the following pattern of consumer price rises from 1970 to 1973.[4]

	%
USA	14·4
Canada	16·0
Japan	24·5
Netherlands	25·2
France	19·9
Germany	18·8
Italy	22·4
UK	26·7

Thus although the UK figure is the highest among this group of countries it is not very much in excess of that for the Netherlands and Japan. However, the gap between UK experience and that of other countries has widened since 1973. UK experience in 1974 was worse than in the other main industrial countries; and in the early months of 1975 UK retail prices were still rising at an annual rate of 20 per cent or so, whereas some countries (notably West Germany) were keeping their increases well below the double-digit level.[5] A major reason for this varying experience is that price rises tended to level off, or to be reversed, in many countries towards the end of 1974, whereas nothing comparable took place in the UK.

It is important to set the recent level of UK inflation in its international context, for it is clear that any explanation which does not refer to experiences elsewhere is unlikely to be satisfactory; and yet, on the other hand, a common worldwide explanation may be of limited relevance to the UK. This topic will engage our attention later.

MECHANICS OF INFLATION

There is a vast literature on the mechanics of inflation; and many disagreements both on theoretical approaches and on empirical tests of such approaches. So we cannot pretend to do more than give the broadest impressions of alternative views.[6]

One view is to put the whole thrust of the explanation in terms of excess demand, so that an increase in spending relative to output potential (or an increase in the rate of growth of output potential) can be said to be *the* reason for inflationary movements at all times and in all places. This explanation can take two different forms. The first is the Keynesian approach, where the prime emphasis is placed on autonomous changes in expenditure, whether private, public or foreign (i.e. for exports). Such changes are assumed to raise incomes not only directly but also through the multiplier process, by which the additional consumption generated at the first round raises incomes still further—with more consumption, more income and so on in succeeding rounds. In its extreme form, this approach is associated with the view that 'money does not matter', i.e. that price and output movements are solely dependent on the spending process outlined above and that the supply of money in a country is of no consequence. This view depends on one (or both) of two extreme assumptions: that interest rates do not rise even though the supply of money is held constant, or that, if interest rates do rise, there is no consequential effect on spending.

The alternative approach to the excess demand explanation is the monetarist one, especially associated with Milton Friedman of the University of Chicago. The emphasis here is placed on the quantity of money relative to the output potential (or the rate of growth of the quantity of money relative to the rate of growth of output potential).

Essentially, the argument is that people hold a given amount of money at a given level of income (in real terms) and so if more money is pumped into the economy they will take steps to convert their additional holdings of money into other assets, thereby driving up the level of activity or prices or both. Whereas the flywheel of the Keynesian approach is the assumption of a stable consumption function (so that there is a clear linkage between autonomous expenditure changes and income changes), the critical assumption in the monetarist approach is that of a stable velocity or demand function for money (so that, assuming velocity quasi-constant, there is a clear linkage between the change in the supply of money and nominal income changes). Corresponding to the extreme Keynesian position that 'money does not matter' there is an extreme monetarist position that 'money is all that matters'.[7] According to this view, an increase in, say, Government spending on goods and services without any increase in the supply of money would be impotent to affect prices or output—essentially on the grounds that the velocity of circulation would stay unchanged or, putting it more technically, that the demand for money is completely inelastic with respect to the rate of interest. So the end result would be that the additional Government spending would drive up interest rates but not the price level or real output. It would also be maintained that there is a 'natural' level of unemployment which is compatible with a steady level of inflation, but that any attempt to keep unemployment below this natural level would imply an *accelerating* rate of inflation.

A second view is that the emphasis should not be placed on excess demand, whether along Keynesian or monetarist lines, but on the costs side of business operations. Costs may rise for various reasons in an economy: it may be a matter of increases in costs of labour, capital or imports or in business taxes. The importance of these various components differs over time; for example, on this approach, rising import costs were very important in the UK late in 1973 but rising labour costs were more important in early 1975. When one asks why these component costs might change, there is a multitude of answers. Thus it can be argued that employee and union attitudes and expectations have changed drastically in recent years, leading to a much more hard-line approach on wage negotiations.[8] Reasons for such a change abound: reversion to earlier militant patterns of behaviour, growth in monopoly power of trade unions,[9] a belief in the entitlement to steady annual growth in real incomes and so on. Whereas belligerency in wage demands has been a matter of steady growth over the years, changes in import costs have been of a more sporadic nature—e.g. the spectacular rises of 1951 and 1973. In so far as import costs push up domestic prices, it is then argued that these rises may be a still further reason for wage demands.

The proponents of the cost-inflation approach differ in the importance that they attach to the money supply. Some would take the line that it is of no importance; even though autonomous cost rises lead to an increase in the demand for money, this demand can be satisfied without increases in interest rates; alternatively, that the increases in interest rates are of no import. Others would take the view that the supply of money has to expand sufficiently to allow the cost increases to do their damnedest, but that the role of money is essentially secondary and accommodating, rather than primary or leading. Furthermore, even though money may have played a part in facilitating increases in output and prices, its role in reversing inflationary developments is deemed to be very limited.[10]

There is obviously much scope for fundamental disagreement in these alternative views; but it is also true that in many cases the differences are more those of emphasis than substance. Before we try to synthesise some of these ideas, let us remind ourselves of what has to be explained.

- Prices have risen in the UK over the whole of the post-war period.
- There has been a marked acceleration of the rate of price rise in recent years, giving rise to fears in many people's minds that we are on the slippery slope to hyperinflation when the rate of price increase is typically much faster than the rate of increase of money supply. Even if there is some doubt about this, it can hardly be denied that inflationary experiences are so ingrained in people's minds that they enter into their views of future developments; in other words, people are less likely to be deceived by money illusion than in the past.
- The more rapid pace of inflation in the 1970s has taken place against a background of higher unemployment levels (at least as measured by the conventional statistics) than in the 1960s. Although particular combinations of rising prices and rising unemployment at particular times can be explained by lags in reactions to monetary and fiscal policies, it seems hard to deny that we do now have a different combination of circumstances from what was accepted as normal only a few years ago.
- Whilst acknowledging that inflation has been a worldwide phenomenon, we still have to explain why Britain's experience has been so much worse than that of other countries, especially in recent years.

Whatever the allegiance to the rival schools of thought, it would seem that three questions have to be answered in seeking to explain the situation in Britain; these questions relate to worker, employer and Government attitudes.

Worker attitudes. The question to ask is why workers demand higher wages without fear of losing their jobs—the traditional check on inordinate wage grabs. The most obvious answer is that post-war history has been such as to foster a general belief that real incomes will grow steadily and that broadly full employment will be maintained in the economy. Furthermore, there have been plenty of examples where the level of employment has been maintained in the face of wage rises, in particular industries, essentially by Government help (e.g. subsidies to the National Coal Board to finance the costs of miners' settlements). So it is a matter not only of thinking that there will be no shortage of jobs in the economy generally but also of believing that there will be no shortage of jobs in one's own industry—and with luck in one's own firm and in one's own locality. In more technical language we can say that even though it is recognised that the supply curve of labour to an industry will be shifted upwards as a result of higher wage awards, the demand curve will be shifted upwards too.

There may also be some further considerations. In so far as we have an expanding industry, any loss of jobs which does take place may well be invisible, in the sense that what is lost is a potential increase of job opportunities rather than any which currently exist. And even if there is a loss of existing jobs, this may well be at the expense of relative newcomers to an industry—and perhaps immigrants—who may count for relatively little in trade union counsels. In other words, if a large rise can be gained for the establishment at the expense of jobs for those on the periphery, then so much the worse for the latter.

Employer attitudes. Why do employers concede large wage increases? The most general answer seems to be that the fear of losses through industrial unrest exceeds the fear of losses from losing business to competitors. This proposition can be expanded in a number of ways. One is that firms, especially capital-intensive ones, will worry about the effect of strikes on their profit record and their ability to raise more capital in future. Another is that if wage demands are being made on a national basis the fear of losing business to domestic competitors is that much less; and there is always the hope, or even expectation, that if foreign competition becomes too uncomfortable some way can be found of mitigating it through import controls, tariffs, 'voluntary' agreements or public subsidies. In technical language we can say that employers, like workers, may feel that demand curves will be shifted upwards to a sufficient extent to offset the upward movement of supply curves and thus avoid the need for substantial cutbacks in their labour force.

Government attitudes. Governments seem to act on the assumption that the supply curve of output to the economy as a whole is quasi-horizontal, so that if fiscal or monetary cutbacks are made the short-term result will be a fall in output and employment rather than in prices.[11] It is also thought, rightly or wrongly, that the immediate electoral disadvantages ('a week is a long time in politics') of large wage and price rises are less than those of large-scale unemployment, even if this is only of short duration. Given these two propositions, it is easy to see why Governments accede to wage and price rises as a lesser evil—perhaps reinforced by the knowledge that revenue gains from progressive taxation are likely to outweigh expenditure additions due to the inflationary process.

To summarise, we would argue that any convincing explanation of inflationary experiences in the UK in recent years must supply answers in terms of attitudes of workers, employers and Government. It can be seen straightaway that this contains elements of both the excess demand and cost explanations, without exclusive reliance on either. It would seem extremely difficult to explain inflation except in the context of a loose enough monetary policy; but that is a very different thing from saying that the money supply is the sole cause of inflation in some deep philosophical sense.

One or two final comments should be made. A general explanation along these lines is sufficiently flexible to allow of differential rates of inflation at different times or in different countries, and so there is no particular problem in analysing recent UK phenomena relative to those of other times or places. Furthermore, if the explanation is a complicated one along lines such as these, it would seem that there is little likelihood of the situation reversing itself quickly. We have taken a long time to get into our present mess, and we are likely to take a long time to get out of it. It is always easier to restrain a horse cantering along gently than one at a full gallop. Now that we have reached a stage where no one under the age of fifty has had any personal experience of living under a régime of falling prices, it is totally unrealistic to think that inflation-minded attitudes can be exorcised overnight.

EFFECTS ON BUSINESS OPERATIONS

Inflation and Business Profitability

Economists have traditionally taken the view that rising prices were good for business and for profits. Thus, for instance, Sir Dennis Robertson argued some fifty years ago[12] that a situation where prices were rising gently was likely to be more conducive to business confidence and investment than one where prices were falling, as they had been at many times in the nineteenth century. And in his *General Theory* Keynes[13] argued that in the upswing of the trade cycle marginal costs would tend to rise relative to average costs as bottlenecks developed, thus shifting the distribution of income away from wages and interest to profits. It is a commonplace proposition in tax theory that the yield of taxes on profits tends to rise more than proportionately to gross national product (GNP) as output and prices rise, simply because of the increasing proportion of profits to GNP

No exponent of the traditional doctrine ever suggested that *all* firms would benefit; there are always bound to be lame ducks. But it was held to apply to *most* firms.

If this proposition were to hold today in anything like this form, business firms would have nothing to worry about; and indeed this book would be unnecessary. But clearly it does not hold; the figures quoted earlier[14] of recent profit experience in the UK are sufficient evidence of that. But if the proposition does not hold, we must ask why this is so; when we have seen the various answers to that question, we can then discuss the most appropriate strategies for business firms.

There would seem to be a number of reasons why the traditional doctrine is not applicable to our present-day economy. The first is that the proposition that 'inflation is good for business' (to put the argument succinctly though crudely) was never meant to apply to the kind of inflationary situation in which we now find ourselves. There is a vast difference between situations where prices rise at rates of, say, 2 per cent per annum and those where prices rise at 20 per cent or more per annum. At worst, the latter case begins to take on connotations of hyperinflation, when the rate of price rises gets hopelessly out of control—as it did in Germany in 1923. It has always been recognised that in this sort of extreme situation, when the unit of monetary account begins to lose all its normal characteristics, there is no hope of maintaining output and employment in any orderly fashion, and so business firms are unlikely to prosper.[15] Even if one takes the more optimistic view that price rises of the order of 20 per cent per annum or so need not end in hyperinflation, one still has to recognise some very serious impediments to business prosperity. One is the sheer degree of uncertainty injected into many business operations—investment planning, financial planning and so on. If prices are to rise by up to 3 per cent per annum or by as little as 1 per cent per annum with a mean expectation of 2 per cent, that is one thing; but it is utterly different if the respective figures are 30 per cent, 10 per cent and 20 per cent. The hazards of entering into long-term commitments, whether in terms of a building programme or a lending programme, are simply not comparable with those when the mean expected price rise is much lower, even though the proportionate variations around the mean may be the same in both cases.

Uncertainty about costs and rates of return induced by very rapidly rising prices may well lead to cutbacks in capital investment programmes and so is one of the reasons why we find inflation and recession together. There may also be squeezes on fixed investment in so far as stock-building pre-empts whatever liquid resources are available. Other reasons for the combination of inflation and recession are associated with the lags in reactions to Government policies. In just the same way as a vehicle continues to travel forward after the brake has been applied, so we find that prices continue to rise after monetary and fiscal action have been taken to cut down the level of demand. Hence the short-term effect of attempts to contain inflation may well be reductions in output and employment whilst, for a time, prices are propelled forward by their existing momentum.

It can also be argued[16] that many increases in taxes, especially those on consumer expenditure, are not a good means of restraining inflation, in that they tend to be cost-inflationary as well as demand-deflationary. The resultant increases in equilibrium price levels may be far from negligible; and thus lead to the conclusion that tax raising may not be the best way to curb inflation.[17]

One other feature of recent inflationary experience is that it has been associated with marked labour unrest. Whatever the causal sequence, the facts are not in dispute. Average number of days lost in industrial disputes in the UK (in millions of days per annum) have been as follows:[18]

1949–52	1·6
1952–67	3·4
1967–70	4·8
1970–73	16·1

Prima facie, it is likely to be difficult to claim that 'inflation is good for business' when the sharp increase in prices between earlier and more recent years has been accompanied by such a sharp escalation of industrial conflict.

So much for some of the ways in which recent inflationary developments have been distinguished from those which were traditionally associated with business prosperity. Another factor to take into account is the immensely greater role of the Government in the economy today. One aspect is taxation. When tax rates are at very low levels the fact that corporation taxes are levied on a profit concept which does not allow for replacement cost of fixed assets or inventories may not be very important; and similarly with personal income tax rates for unincorporated businesses[19] or taxation of nominal capital gains for any type of business. But when business firms have to face tax rates at modern levels, and inflation is proceeding apace, the situation is entirely different. Referring back to Table 1.2 (p. 2) we can see the drastic effects of inflation plus taxation on UK corporate profits in 1974 compared to earlier years; and, in particular, the ruinous effect of the full liability to tax of stock appreciation. Even though *ad hoc* relief may be given by a Chancellor, as in November 1974,[20] the basic truth remains that increasing tax liabilities may more than offset the notional advantages of inflation in generating higher business profits.

Another aspect of increasing Government intervention is the likelihood of price and profit controls. We have seen in the post-war period increasingly complex systems of Government control, ranging from earlier appeals for wages restraint, to policies embracing all types of incomes, thence to price controls and finally to the whole sophisticated armoury of the counter-inflation legislation of the Conservative Government in the period from late 1972 to early 1974. It is beyond our scope here to discuss the political implications and tendencies inherent in setting up statutory bodies with enormous powers, but it is nonetheless worth remembering an extremely prescient (and totally neglected) warning given by the late Sir Dennis Robertson[21] as long ago as 1960:

> I should like to know more about how the assembly which fixes it [the upward movement of the wages scale] is to be composed and how wide its jurisdiction is to extend. Only over money, wages and salaries, everything else being given? or will it want to have a say about prices? profits? dividend policy? some at least of the social services? Taxation—traditionally a subject at the very heart of the business of democratic Parliament? Are we getting rather uncomfortably near the Fascist or Falangist idea of a powerful functional or corporative assembly in almost permanent session perhaps at Church House, leaving the political House of Commons across the road an embarrassing surplus of time in which to discuss such subjects as corporal punishment and strip-tease clubs?

Comment is superfluous.

As for the economic aspects of such controls, there are several lessons. One is the increasing tendency over the post-war period to impose price freezes or limitations. When allied with an absence of similar controls on wages and salaries, as in the latter part of 1974, this is a perfect recipe for the destruction and annihilation of business profits. Even when the conjunction of circumstances is not as extreme as this a complex apparatus of control is bound to incorporate arbitrary elements, thus generating a sense of unfairness ('divisiveness' in popular idiom) between different industries and different enterprises. Another effect is the multiplication of uncertainties; if a business firm simply cannot be sure that it will be allowed to reap the commercial benefit of some risky activity because of the danger of a Government clampdown, then there is all the less motivation for undertaking such ventures.

So it can be seen that there are some weighty reasons why inflation today is unlikely to result in a straightforward boom to business firms. The nature of recent inflationary developments is very different from that associated with the upturn of the traditional business cycle; and Government intervention by fiscal or other means is likely to be such as to erode rather than enhance profitability. There are many other factors which must be noted, albeit briefly. A higher than average rate of inflation in one country may have adverse repercussions. Unless exchange rates are allowed to adjust, sales to foreigners will become more difficult and purchases from foreigners will become more tempting. Foreign willingness to invest funds in such a country may also be tempered by fears of future depreciation, dividend controls and the like. Nor should one underestimate the sheer nuisance value and administrative chores of coping with inflation—more frequent wage negotiations, price revisions, issues of price lists, catalogues and the like.

To conclude this section of the argument, it is worth referring to a study of the effects of recent inflation on business financing and investment in the case of the Post Office telecommunications business.[22] The main points were as follows:

- The telecommunications business is a large one, with annual expenditure totalling some £1200 million on current account and £700 million on fixed assets. Some 65 per cent of the current account expenditure is directly affected by inflationary pressures.
- A profit of £61 million in 1969–70 had become a loss of £61 million by 1973–4; and whereas the rate of return on capital was 8·4 per cent in 1969–70 (more or less on target) it had sunk to 6·4 per cent in 1973–4.
- Important components of additional costs due to inflation were the need for supplementing depreciation provisions and pension funding.
- Despite some limited increases in tariffs and productivity improvement, much additional borrowing was needed to provide the necessary funds.
- The short-term gains (for prices and incomes policy) from delays in raising tariffs were far outweighed by the long-term disadvantages of, for example, stimulation of consumption (and hence the need for more investment) and much sharper eventual tariff increases.
- The short-term cutbacks in investment were likely to lead to plant imbalances in the future, in that only some types of capital expenditure could readily be restricted.

APPROPRIATE BUSINESS REACTIONS

The situation faced by business firms over the foreseeable future must be one of rising prices, even if the pace is somewhat less than that experienced in 1974 and 1975, in the aftermath of the world oil price rise. In formulating some general principles of conduct one must make a prior assumption about the way in which Government is most likely to operate. We shall assume that something like the present pattern persists: a half-hearted attempt to hold back inflation by a mixture of traditional fiscal and monetary policy, voluntary persuasion such as the 'Social Contract', and discriminatory intervention at selected points, on such lines as those set out in the Government's paper on 'The Attack on Inflation'.[23]

The first canon of behaviour is political and not economic. In a world where Government decisions are very frequently taken in response to the shrill cries or threatening menaces of pressure groups operating at parliamentary or Civil Service levels, business enterprises clearly cannot afford that their voices be unheard in such jamborees. Much as one may deplore this method of regulating or conducting the economy of the country, it would be foolish to ignore its importance in contemporary life. There are, in fact, two sides to any such representations. The first is simply to reiterate, and reiterate, and reiterate the central proposition that businessmen are in business to make profits; that it is the making of profits that makes an economy tick and, by and large, makes everyone better off. There should therefore be no truck with the age-old confidence trick of voluntarily agreeing to pass up profits for some alleged benefit to Society at large. All the evidence suggests that actions of this sort are neither good for business nor good for the economy, except in the most ephemeral of senses. It might, in fact, be a good business motto to argue that although a week may be a long time in politics it is a short time in business. The second aspect of representation to the authorities is to make one's voice heard about particular legislative measures which may compel business to act in one way rather than another. This may be a matter of monetary policy, fiscal policy or direct controls of one kind or another. Given the tendentious advice which is often offered on such subjects, and the seemingly persistent inability or unwillingness of the authorities to distinguish between sensible and foolish views, it is clearly a matter of elementary self-protection to make one's voice heard in such matters.

So much for action at the political level. There is no doubt a great deal more to be said about the details of such representations, but we do not claim to have the necessary expertise, time or space to discuss them. So let us now turn to more purely economic actions. The most important proposition is that one has to learn to think all the time in real rather than nominal terms. This is easy to enunciate as a general principle but very hard to live up to in practice, given the compelling forces of custom and habit. An immediate implication is that one must have systems of management and financial accounting which take account of price changes in respect of fixed assets, inventories, debtors and creditors and so on. It is not part of our purpose here to survey the rival merits of the current purchasing power (CPP) accounting approach (using the index of retail prices for all adjustments)[24] or of specific price indicators for different types of assets—more especially as the report of the Sandilands Committee is still to come at the time of writing.[25] All we are concerned with is the proposition that accounting in nominal terms may be at best misleading and at worst disastrous in times of rapid inflation.

Nor is it simply a matter of applying the real terms principle to what has already happened. Many decisions on many different subjects may be crucially and critically affected by the application of the principle. Decisions about investment plans, the likely return after allowing for price rises of inputs and outputs, the rising current costs likely to be associated with more and less labour-intensive methods of production, and the real as distinct from the money costs of interest on borrowings must all be thought of in this context. It is easy enough to put forward the general principle that under inflationary conditions one is likely to be at an advantage if one increases one's physical assets and indebtedness, rather than being a holder of liquid assets; but the detailed pursuit of any such policy calls for unremitting attention to many variables.

There are other aspects of future policy which also call for thought. One obvious point is to avoid like the plague commitment to fixed-price sales contracts in times of rapidly rising prices. Programmes which of necessity take several years to execute become inherently more risky. What may appear to be a perfectly viable proposal at present may cease to be so once prices of own inputs or other outputs have doubled or trebled—and the cardinal rule of compound interest, that prices rising at 20 per cent per annum double in less than four years, must never be forgotten. Another is the attitude towards exports: one tends to think of exports as a more risky activity and less of a soft option than home sales. But if we are in for an era of arbitrary Government intervention with prices, profit margins, etc. on home sales, it may be much less risky and uncertain to engage in export activities which are not subject to such intervention, at least in one's own country.

Although it is trite enough to say that businessmen must be quick on their toes and flexible enough to adapt to rapidly changing circumstances, the arguments for such observations do seem stronger than ever in an era of rapidly rising prices. One obvious aspect is the danger that a firm's liquidity position (in the sense of the ratio of liquid assets to short-term debt) may deteriorate surprisingly sharply in the face of untoward events (as happened as a consequence of the great rises in prices of materials in the first half of 1974).[26] Another is that the frequency with which prices of products are adjusted may need to be much greater. Once per annum may be sufficient if prices are rising at, say, 5 per cent per annum, but it is certainly not when the 20 per cent per annum mark is reached. Most commentators are not in the habit of handing out bouquets to the UK car industry, but the frequency with which it raised the prices of its products in 1974 and 1975 is entirely understandable. Nor should it be thought that infrequent larger rises are a good substitute for frequent small ones; the former is only too likely to attract adverse public attention.

Speedy reactions are necessary in many other ways (e.g. switching between products, components and markets), but we have said sufficient to illustrate the principles involved. Which firms are most likely to survive, or survive profitably, in these circumstances is a nice question. Small firms are traditionally alleged to have advantages in speed of manoeuvre; they may also attract much less attention from Government price or profit inspectors hungry for red meat. On the other hand, they can easily be swamped by a tidal wave of illiquidity.

NOTES AND REFERENCES

1. Cf. M. C. Kennedy, 'The Economy as a Whole', in A. R. Prest and D. J. Coppock (eds.), *The UK Economy*, 5th edition, Weidenfeld and Nicholson (London, 1974), p. 38.
2. See, for example, G. J. Burgess and A. J. Webb, 'The Profits of British Industry', *Lloyd's Bank Review*, April 1974, and M. A. King, 'The United Kingdom Profits Crisis: Myth or Reality?', *The Economic Journal*, March 1975.
3. And even though cash flow was better in the second half of the year it was insufficient to finance as much as 50 per cent of capital expenditure, with consequential additional borrowing, reductions in trade credit and the like (*Bank of England Quarterly Bulletin*, March 1975).
4. From *National Economic Review*, November 1974. Although later figures (ibid., August 1975) show that over the period 1970–4 Japan had the largest percentage price rise and the UK the second largest the argument in the text still holds.
5. See *OECD Economic Indicators*, March 1975, for details. Also *National Institute Economic Review*, February 1975.
6. For a more detailed summary, see A. S. Blinder and R. M. Solow, 'Analytical Foundations of Fiscal Policy', in *The Economics of Public Finance*, Brookings Institution (Washington, DC, 1974).
7. It is not always accepted that this phraseology is a fair summary. See A. S. Blinder and R. M. Solow, *op. cit.*, p. 59.
8. See E. H. Phelps Brown, 'A Non-Monetary View of the Pay Explosion', *Three Banks Review*, March 1975.
9. Note that it is much more a matter of the *growth* of monopoly power of unions, rather than its absolute *level*. Cf. E. H. Phelps Brown, *op. cit.*, p. 21.
10. 'Even if we believe that it was a rapid increase in the supply of money that let the genie out of the bottle, we can hardly believe that a slower increase will get it back again.' Cf. E. H. Phelps Brown, *op. cit.* p. 21.
11. It may also be thought that the cost-raising effects of tax or interest rate increases may outweigh their demand-reducing effects; although the same reasoning would not apply, at least in a simple form, to public expenditure decreases.
12. D. H. Robertson, *Money*, Nisbet, Cambridge University Press, 2nd edition (Cambridge, 1924), p. 123.
13. J. M. Keynes, *The General Theory of Employment, Interest and Money*, Macmillan (London, 1936), p. 299.
14. p. 3 *supra*. See also *National Institute Review*, February 1975, pp. 34 ff., for further corroboration.
15. Thus, steel production fell from 12 to 6 million tons per annum in Germany between 1922 and 1923; and the unemployment percentage rose from 2·8 to 28·2.
16. For a recent discussion, see A. S. Blinder and R. M. Solow, *op. cit.* p. 98 ff.
17. Ibid., p. 101.
18. Cf. M. C. Kennedy, *op. cit.*, p. 39.
19. There are, in fact, two different points here. One is the inadequacy of original cost for fixed assets and inventories; the other is the increasingly heavy weight of a progressive tax rate structure as prices and incomes rise through time, but tax

allowances and starting points for different tax rate bands remain unchanged in money terms (and hence fall in real terms).

20. Stock appreciation for corporation tax purposes for 1973–4 was limited to 10 per cent of trading profits (before deduction of capital allowances); price controls were eased; and additional medium-term funds were made available for investment. This method of relief was extended in the April 1975 Budget.
21. Dennis Robertson, *Growth, Wages, Money*, Cambridge University Press (Cambridge, 1961), p. 42.
22. *Public Expenditure, Inflation and the Balance of Payments*, Ninth Report from the Expenditure Committee, 1974 Session, HC 328, July 1974, Appendix 3.
23. *The Attack on Inflation*, Cmnd 6151, HMSO (London, 1975).
24. See as examples the annual accounts published by ICI and Grand Metropolitan in March 1975; in both cases CPP profits were very different to conventional computations, although, as it happened, in opposite directions.
25. *Inflation Accounting*, Cmnd 6225, HMSO (London, 1975), called for a new system of current cost accounting (as opposed to historic cost accounting). This would particularly affect the entries for stocks and the depreciation of fixed assets.
26. *The National Institute Review*, November 1974, p. 21, shows that for industrial and commercial companies the ratio of selected liquid assets to bank advances fell from about 1·2 in 1963 to 0·75 in 1973 and to 0·6 in the second quarter of 1974.

    See also *The Times*, 12 March 1975, for an account of the liquidity problems of three large companies—British Oxygen, Imperial Tobacco and Turner & Newall. Cash preservation was said to be the overriding objective; the methods included cuts in investment programmes, trade debts, stocks and the labour force. In the case of Turner & Newall, it was also reported that thirty to forty accountants were needed to cope with price controls alone.

    The Ryder Report (*British Leyland: The Next Decade*, HMSO, April 1975) is another valuable source of information on these problems.

CHAPTER 2

Indexation

SAMUEL BRITTAN AND PETER LILLEY

Whether or not inflation is, as Milton Friedman puts it, 'everywhere and always a monetary phenomenon' used to be a subject of debate. What has never been disputed, however, is that inflation is of its very nature an 'anti-monetary' phenomenon: it erodes the value and undermines the usefulness of money.

One of the major functions of money in an advanced economy is to act as a standard of value over periods of time. Contracts, loans, rules, regulations and tax rates are almost automatically denominated in money. But if the value of money changes because of a general rise in prices and costs unanticipated by those who entered into the contract or who framed the regulation, their original purpose is to some extent thwarted.

Inevitably, therefore, inflation generates demands for a more constant standard of value over time than money. The obvious alternative standard of value is some unit of constant general purchasing power based on a comprehensive index of prices of goods and services. If such an index is not available contracts may be denominated in terms of the cost of a smaller bundle of goods or even in units of a single physical commodity.

The present worldwide inflation has naturally generated considerable interest in indexation (which is the general term for the replacement of money by some other standard of value over time). However, this interest is far from new. The subject has been of lively concern to many of the classical economic writers since at least the beginning of the nineteenth century.[1] Lowe, Jevons, Marshall and Keynes all advocated some use of indexation, or the 'tabular standard' as it was known (in reference to the use of *tables* of variations in purchasing power). Bagehot and Griffen were among those who opposed the introduction of indexation. Moreover, the historic interest has not just occurred during periods of generally rising prices; indexing has also been of much concern when prices have been falling.

Nor has interest in indexation been purely theoretical. Various forms of indexation have been practised in a large number of countries over many centuries. The earliest examples were merely contracts requiring payment in kind—for example, the payment of tithes in corn. Since the regular publication of price indices became prevalent, indexation of loans, mortgages, wage contracts, social security benefits, tax schedules and most other forms of contract have been tried in countries ranging from Belgium and Brazil to Israel and the USA.

Despite this long history and widespread use of indexation the argument about it is still remarkably inconclusive. Economists and politicians still disagree among themselves about its overall impact on the management of inflation, its practical desirability in specific areas and the politico-moral implications of its widespread introduction. In the three sections below we examine respectively the macroeconomic, microeconomic and political controversies about indexation.

MACROECONOMIC EFFECTS OF INDEXATION

Since the revival of interest in indexation has been provoked by our current inflation, the principal economic argument has been about the impact indexation would have on the *rate* of inflation.

Some economists allege that widespread indexation would aggravate inflation, others that its effect would be neutral but that it would help us to live with a given rate of inflation, and yet others that it would make the cure of inflation easier.

Which of these three schools of thought is correct, and how can such apparently conflicting theories continue to be propounded after centuries of argument and wide practical experience?

The answer is that all three theories are correct! Indexation can aggravate inflation, be neutral or help to cure it. Which of these three results follows from the introduction of indexation depends on the budgetary and monetary policies which accompany it. If a Government persists in pursuing an unstable inflationary financial policy, then indexation will exacerbate the inflationary impact of that policy. If the Government is pursuing a neutral financial policy,[2] the effect of indexation will be fairly neutral. Whereas if the Government is pursuing a disinflationary financial policy, indexation will help mitigate the unpleasant deflationary side effects.

The reason that the debate about the impact of indexation has resulted in apparently irreconcilable conclusions is simply that the disputants too rarely spell out the nature of the Government's financial policies which they are tacitly assuming will accompany indexation. Indeed, all too often those who discuss the issue are not consciously aware that they are (unavoidably) making some implicit assumption about Government financial policy!

Indexation does not produce such apparently different consequences by operating differently according to the financial policy pursued by the

Government. On the contrary, indexation does precisely the same thing in each case: it makes a given change in monetary demand have a larger immediate effect on money prices and costs and a smaller effect on the volume of output and employment.

In an economy where prices and wages are mainly not indexed an inflationary (or, as it is politely called, 'expansionary') Government financial policy results in an immediate boom in the volume of output and employment. This is followed only after some delay by an acceleration in prices, wages and other costs. Likewise a disinflationary (or deflationary) financial policy usually results in an immediate reduction in output and employment, followed only after some delay by a moderation of price and wage inflation. Politicians tend to like inflationary financial policies precisely because they induce an immediate boom while their inevitable effect on prices is delayed (for example, until after an election is over). Likewise, politicians flinch from disinflationary policies because their immediate effect is on output and employment and their beneficial effect on inflation may not appear until later (when the Government may have been swept from office).

The important thing to understand, however, is this: the only reason Government 'expansionary' policies normally affect the level of output and employment is that prices and wages are slow to respond to a change in the level of demand. Likewise, the only reason disinflationary policies induce a temporary depression in output and employment is that prices and wages do not respond immediately.

Since indexation goes some way towards making prices and costs respond more rapidly to changes in the level of demand, it can help an economy to avoid booms and slumps. If the Government increases monetary spending in a fully indexed economy it would result in immediate, instead of delayed, price acceleration with less of a boom. An indexed economy would also experience more rapid moderation of price and wage increases, with less of a depression, if the Government follows deflationary policies.

For those readers who wisely distrust such abstract summaries of complex phenomena it is worth spelling out the steps by which, for example, a deflationary policy would affect an unindexed and a fully indexed economy.

Suppose the Government reduces monetary demand by raising taxes.[3] With less money in their pay packets, people will spend less. The prices of flexibly priced goods (like fresh vegetables) will fall immediately, without any loss of output. But the prices of most other products and services will, in a non-indexed economy, remain unchanged. People will nonetheless of necessity spend less, so the volume of output will fall. Less overtime will be worked, fewer employees will be taken on, others will be sacked and some firms will be bankrupted. However, it will not be until the next round of wage negotiations that the reduced bargaining power of labour will be reflected in some moderation of wage settlements. Given smaller wage increases, manufacturers will subsequently be able (and encouraged by waning demand) to increase the prices of their products by less than they would otherwise have done. Thus deflation in an unindexed economy produces first a drop in output and employment and only subsequently a deceleration in prices and wages.

In a largely indexed economy this pattern of events would be compressed. The initial drop in monetary spending (as a result of increased taxes) would still produce an immediate drop only in the prices of flexibly priced goods, such as fresh vegetables. However, this would be transmitted to the consumer price index, which would therefore fall or register a smaller increase. This would soon be reflected in all indexed prices, wages, loans and other costs when they are adjusted (usually monthly). Consequently, manufacturers will find their costs slightly reduced. Since they will be facing reduced demand some firms will pass lower costs on in slightly lower prices. Others will be enabled to avoid bankruptcy. Price cuts will feed back into the consumer price index and thereby into a further reduction of indexed prices and costs. Thus indexation will bring about a more rapid decline in price and wage inflation with fewer bankruptcies, less unemployment and a smaller drop in output. (The effect of outside 'shocks' etc. in delaying this process are discussed on pp. 30–1.)

The process by which initial price reductions feed back into the price index, producing a secondary round of reductions in indexed prices, may seem alarming at first sight. It sounds as if a small initial drop in monetary demand in an indexed economy could send prices spiralling down indefinitely. Even more frighteningly, a small inflationary increase in demand could apparently send prices spiralling up without limit. In fact, this cannot and does not happen. The process of feedback is, in mathematical jargon, 'highly convergent'. It can be shown rigorously that even if all non-flexible prices and costs were fully indexed (an almost inconceivable, though possibly desirable, state of affairs) successive rounds of indexed price changes would be smaller and smaller. And even if the process continued indefinitely it would result only in moving the general price level by the same percentage as the initial increase in flexible prices. This is roughly what would have happened over a much longer period if the economy had *not* been indexed.

It would be wrong to pretend that indexation would make deflation entirely painless and simple. In the first place it is inconceivable that *all* prices and costs could be indexed. Second, there is bound to be a delay before the reduction in demand has fully fed through to indexed prices. Because of that delay output and employment would still take some of the brunt of deflation. Third, inflation does not only affect the overall price level, it also distorts relative prices and the pattern of production. Consequently deflation is bound to be accompanied by the strains inherent in any readjustment of relative prices and of the structure of production. Indexation cannot take care of that.

One argument frequently adduced for supposing that the introduction of indexation would exacerbate inflation is that 'it would amount to a declaration of surrender'. This argument presumes that the only purpose of introducing indexation is to help live with inflation. The populace would therefore deduce that the Government had abandoned plans to reduce the rate of inflation. Any who were previously expecting a decline in the rate of inflation would therefore probably revise their expectations. So the average expected inflation rate would rise. Since expectations feed into the inflation rate, at least in the short term, the mere introduction of indexation could cause inflation to accelerate.

The argument is plausible. And, indeed, if the Government had decided to abandon the fight against inflation and was introducing indexation in the hope of making inflation easier to live with, the popular reaction postulated in this argument would be entirely rational. However, if the populace does collectively possess this sophisticated understanding of economic policy measures, the average expectations of inflation would presumably decline should indexation be introduced in the context of a renewed *de*flationary policy.

Of course, if indexing could make unrestrained inflation tolerable for everybody it would scarcely matter whether or not the official sponsorship of indexation marginally increased inflationary expectations. Unfortunately, the most that can be hoped for from indexation as an aid to living with continuing inflation is that it will remove some *unnecessary* risk associated with inflation. Thus if people had the opportunity to enter into indexed contracts they would not be obliged to gamble on the future rate of inflation, as they are every time they sign a contract denominated in money. This in itself is a substantial advantage. The extent and potential for indexing private contracts to obtain this advantage are discussed in the next section.

However, inflation will still be unpleasantly uncertain[4] and risky even if indexation is employed in all private contracts. This is because unanticipated movements in the general level of prices are symptoms and consequences of unanticipated changes in monetary demand. These are bound to be disruptive of business and to cause arbitrary (though not necessarily unintended) transfers of wealth from one section of the population to another.

Only to the extent that the Government itself enters into (and abides by) indexed contracts may the unexpected disturbances of inflation be reduced. But this is simply because the Government would thereby limit its own freedom of action. For example, if the Government had always issued only indexed gilt-edged securities, holders of the national debt would not have suffered the frequent unanticipated real losses they have incurred since the war. As to whether or not there would have been a net reduction in insecurity and unanticipated loss across the economy as a whole it is impossible to say. It may be that holders of indexed gilt-edged securities would merely have been protected at the expense of some other group. The implications of indexation of Government transactions are discussed in more detail in the final section of this chapter.[5]

MICROECONOMICS OF INDEXATION IN THE PRIVATE SECTOR

Given that indexation of private contracts is in general desirable (at least in conjunction with a disinflationary budgetary policy), why does it not happen spontaneously?

The answer is that in many areas some form of indexation or its equivalent does occur spontaneously once awareness of inflation becomes widespread. Already in the UK almost all long-term construction programmes, capital projects and supply contracts, for example, have cost escalator clauses. This is a direct result of the burnt fingers suffered by many suppliers in the 1960s when accelerating inflation (coupled with unstable exchange rates) made fixed-price contracts hopelessly unprofitable. Customers have been willing to accept some form of escalator clause because they realise that their own unit revenues will be rising roughly *par passu* with suppliers' unit costs. Similarly, most business rents have regular reviews, and commercial rents are often effectively indexed by being related to the revenue of the business. Many wage contracts have cost-of-living clauses built in. A widespread substitute for indexation is a tendency to shorten the length of contracts or to make specific allowance for periodic adjustment.

Nonetheless, it remains true that formal indexation remains far less widespread than its theoretical advantages suggest would be likely. In particular, indexed loans are virtually non-existent, many wage contracts still contain no cost-of-living clauses, and tax schedules and other State regulations rarely contain any automatic adjustment for monetary depreciation.

This is partly because there are genuine costs involved in denominating contracts in terms of an index instead of in money. Each party to a contract must evaluate the likely impact of alternative indices and then agreement must be reached on which index is to be used. Subsequently payments must constantly be recalculated, and the company may have to adjust its other costs and prices to keep them in line. Even the constant remarking of prices, adjusting of invoices and revising of sales literature to accord with variations in indexed costs and prices can be exceedingly expensive. That is one reason why it is desirable to return to a stable, universally acceptable monetary standard.

But there are other impediments in the way of wider usage of indexation which are not inherent to it. It is easiest to consider them in the context of each of the main types of contract where indexation is not yet as widespread as might be expected—business loans, mortgages and wages.

Business Loans and Securities

There are two principal types of indexed security. The most common type adjusts the interest payment each year to keep it constant in purchasing-power terms; when repayment is made the initial principal is also adjusted for intervening price increases. The alternative type of indexed security involves the payment each year of a constant money interest rate *plus* the rate of inflation experienced during the year. This compensates for depreciation of capital as it occurs, so the original money principal is repayed at the end of the loan period without further adjustment.

The two types of loan are illustrated below.

Table 2.1 Alternative Types of Indexed Security
Example: £1000 lent in 1970 for 5 years at a 2% real rate of interest.

	UK CONSUMER PRICE INDEX		TYPE 1	TYPE 2
Year	*Index*	*Change on previous year*	*Interest payments*	
1970	100·0	—	—	—
1971	109·4	+9·4%	£21·88	£114
1972	117·2	+7·1%	£23·44	£91
1973	128·0	+9·2%	£25·60	£112
1974	148·5	+16·0%	£29·70	£180
1975	184·4	+24·2%	£36·88	£262
			Repayment of principal	
			£1844	£1000

Both are equivalent in real terms and they cost the same as an unindexed loan yielding a flat 15·0 per cent per annum (i.e. 2 per cent plus the average rate of inflation, which was 13·0 per cent per annum during the period).

Experience in most countries suggests that type 1 is most popular with both borrowers and lenders since it combines stable real income with guaranteed return of capital. Type 2 involves unpredictable variations in annual income which are unlikely to be desired by the lender or easily financed by the borrower.

However, in the UK type 1 loans suffer a significant tax disadvantage relative to both type 2 and an unindexed loan of equivalent real cost. This is because the difference in money terms between the principal and the repayment of principal must be paid out of after-tax income. Annual interest, by contrast, can be offset against tax. Thus at a 52 per cent corporate tax rate a company would need to earn £1896 profit to pay the interest on a type 1 indexed loan, whereas a fixed-interest loan of equivalent real interest rate would need only £750 of profit over the period.

It is scarcely surprising, therefore, that virtually no company in the UK has issued an index-linked security. If indexed loans are to be facilitated the Government must alter the tax position to remove this distortion.

There are also institutional reasons which discourage companies from issuing indexed securities. For example, the articles of association or loan trust deeds of many companies put limits on their potential indebtedness. Since the money value of principal requiring repayment under an indexed loan will rise with the rate of inflation, a company could find itself infringing its own trust deeds merely because of an acceleration in the rate of inflation. Obviously the company could alter its articles or deeds if it could obtain the agreements of its shareholders, but this is a bothersome process.

Financial institutions, as against operating companies, face an even stronger disincentive against indexing their securities. Financial institutions endeavour largely to match the term, risk and form of their liabilities with the term, risk and form of their assets. They can thus only prudently offer indexed loans if they can match these against indexed assets. The assets which comprise the bulk of the assets held by financial institutions are securities issued by either Government or (to a lesser extent) private companies. So until Government or private industry issues indexed securities none of the financial institutions (pension funds, life assurance offices, banks, etc.) will be able to offer indexed securities. In practice, the onus is upon Government to create indexed securities in which financial institutions may invest, since many are legally obliged to place a large portion of their funds in Government securities. Until an indexed gilt-edged security is available, no indexed pensions or life assurance policies will be available to the private individual.

Strangely enough, these tax and institutional disadvantages are rarely given as the explanation of why companies do not issue indexed loans. It is more common to refer to the 'risk' companies would run if they indexed their loans. 'Suppose the rate of inflation accelerates', it is often argued, 'how could the company afford to repay the inflation-adjusted principal?' Undoubtedly many businessmen have been dissuaded from considering indexed loans by this kind of argument. But in fact it incorporates three fallacies.

First, it ignores the fact that the company's own selling prices and revenues will, over the lengthy period of the loan, roughly keep in line with the average level of prices. So if inflation accelerates, the company should have higher money profits from which to finance repayment of inflation-adjusted principal.

Second, it ignores the fact that lenders, too, will presumably perceive a similar risk of inflation accelerating. If the loan is not indexed the lenders therefore face the prospect of the purchasing power of their capital being wiped out. The prospect of accelerating inflation is therefore as likely to induce lenders to refuse to lend at fixed interest as it is to provoke borrowers to refuse to offer indexed securities. In fact, of course, markets do not work in terms of such blanket refusals. Any form of security may be attractive *at a price*. Presumably lenders would be prepared to accept a lower (maybe even negative) initial rate of return than they would require on a fixed-interest unindexed security if the loan was protected against inflation. This should be sufficient to persuade some borrowers to issue such a security even though it would mean forgoing the prospect of real profit in the event of accelerating inflation.

Third, it ignores the fact that there is always a possibility that the rate of inflation will decline. If it does, companies will find their margins squeezed in money and even in real terms. Companies which have borrowed at a fixed money rate of interest set at a level which reflected higher rates of inflation may be bankrupted by the burden of interest. This is the classic cause of bankruptcy during unexpected deflationary periods. By contrast, a company with an indexed loan will be protected by the fact that the money cost of servicing the loan declines automatically with the rate of inflation.

In short, the fixed-interest bond is *more* risky for both lender and borrower than an indexed bond. Businesses which borrow at a fixed rate are gambling on the prospect of an acceleration in the rate of inflation. Savers who lend at a fixed rate are gambling that inflation will come down. Since the late 1950s borrowers have, in fact, consistently won their bet and lenders have correspondingly lost. At some stage in the future, however, if any Government really does conquer inflation, the situation may be reversed. Indexed loans avoid the necessity of gambling on the rate of price inflation and leave companies exposed only to the much smaller variations in the real rate of interest.

In the absence of indexation high and unstable rates of inflation destroy the normal long-term capital market. Any long-term unindexed loan is a gamble on the future rate of inflation—which is inherently unpredictable over the long term.

Gamblers apart, people will prefer to limit their risk by lending and borrowing short term. This is the major reason why long-term fixed-interest lending as a proportion of total lending has declined over the last decade. Nowadays many long-term industrial projects are financed under long-term borrowing arrangements with a variable interest rate related to the *short-term* money rate. For example, one of the largest private projects ever financed in the UK—the Forties Oil Field in the North Sea, for which £420 million was raised—has been financed under such an arrangement. This form of financing is virtually a form of indexation. It is similar to the type 2 loan illustrated in Table 2.1 on p. 23. The interest rate varies over the life of the loan. However, in the type 2 indexed loan the interest rate is related directly to the rate of inflation, whereas in the Forties type of financing it is related to the short-term interest rate, which is only indirectly linked to the rate of inflation.

Mortgages

Mortgages are a special kind of loan which merit separate consideration. They are both held and financed by a very large number of individuals. This makes them a very sensitive political issue.

The mortgage holder has been one of the principal beneficiaries of inflation. He has profited from it in two ways. First, the cost of servicing his mortgage has lagged well behind the rise in value of his house. Second, an increasing proportion of the cost of servicing his mortgage has become eligible for tax relief. However, inflation has also led to higher nominal interest rates (albeit negative in real terms), which has the effect of making the cost of servicing a mortgage artificially high in relation to income in early years and artificially low in later years. This has effectively prevented some potential home owners from taking on mortgages.

In contrast to the mortgage holder, the building society depositor has been one of the major sufferers from inflation. His capital has been eroded by inflation, and the interest which it has earned has been artificially depressed so that it reflects the rate of inflation even less than interest rates of other savings media. This has been achieved partly by collective action by the building societies at the behest of the Government, partly by an injection of Government funds and partly by controls on interest rates in competing savings media (like bank deposits) to which small investors have access. Moreover, the depositor has in effect been paying tax on his interest rate even though it is a grossly inadequate compensation for the depreciating value of his deposit.

Doubtless there has sometimes been an element of rough justice in this pattern of gains and losses. The building society depositor is often a future or past mortgage holder. But the justice is extremely rough since gains do not automatically match losses. Many depositors who are in effect subsidising the house buyer are elderly people who were never themselves able to afford to buy a house. Moreover, those depositors who are potential house buyers have found it more difficult to accumulate the deposit for a house since their savings with the building societies have been constantly eroded.

Indexation of mortgage loans, deposits and the tax system would have reduced but by no means eliminated these distortions and injustices. In particular indexation would not of necessity lead to payment of a positive real interest rate. Depositors have 'freely' continued to leave their money with the building societies at nominal interest rates which have been consistently below the rate of inflation simply because superior investment opportunities were only fleetingly available. In these circumstances they would presumably continue to deposit their funds with the building societies even if deposits were indexed at a negative rate. Indeed, small savers might prefer the security of knowing that their real capital would not be eroded by more than, say, 10 per cent per annum to the uncertain possibility that the rate of inflation (on their best guess) would only exceed the interest rate on some unindexed deposit by, say, 8 per cent. In any case, so long as the building society can offer negative real rates on its indexed deposits it can also charge negative real rates on indexed loans.

In practice, however, the building societies do not offer to index deposits or, *a fortiori*, their mortgage loans. This is doubtless partly because they would be too ashamed to admit in black and white that they had no intention of reimbursing depositors the full real value of their deposits. More important is the unindexed tax treatment of interest rates. As mentioned above, high nominal interest rates, which are in fact less than adequate to compensate for erosion of real purchasing power of the loan, can be offset against tax. But if a real interest rate (possibly negative) is charged separately and the money value of the loan outstanding is revalued to compensate for loss of purchasing power, the extra money cost of repaying capital could not be offset against tax.

This distortion would be eliminated if the tax system were indexed. Indexation of the tax treatment of interest would mean that only the real rate of interest (if positive) would be eligible for tax relief or liable to taxation. In practice, the real rate of interest (i.e. the difference between the interest rate and the percentage increase in the general price level) has been negative in recent years. So indexation would have eliminated both tax relief for mortgage holders and tax levied on depositors' interest.

Almost inevitably, the indexation of the tax treatment of interest on mortgages would raise the cost of mortgages to the mortgage holder. If unaccompanied by other measures, it would increase the monthly repayment required from a mortgage holder who is in the first year of his mortgage and paying tax at the standard rate by as much as 40 per cent. Mortgage payers who were nearing the end of their loan would see a far smaller proportionate increase in their annual repayments, since the bulk of these are deemed to be capital rather than interest.

However, if the mortgage loan itself was indexed this would substantially alter the profile of payments over the life of the loan. Instead of paying a very large proportion of income in early years and a low proportion of income towards the end of the loan the pattern would be more even. The reduction in payments required in early life as a result of indexing the loan would on realistic assumptions be greater than the increase in payments in early years that would result from indexing tax treatment of interest rates. Over the life of the loan the mortgage payer would be worse off as a result of comprehensive indexation. He would certainly pay more tax (thereby, one hopes, permitting a small reduction in the general level of tax rates). And if indexation were used to abolish negative real interest rates he would also pay back more in real terms to the building society. But he would be subject to less financial strain in the early days of home ownership. As a result fewer low-income potential first-time buyers would be unnecessarily excluded from taking out a mortgage.

The scheme of indexation of mortgages envisaged above is known as the 'real value mortgage' scheme. It is analagous to the type 1 indexed business loan outlined above. There are many minor variants but basically all involve revaluing the outstanding loan at the beginning of each year. Interest is then charged on the revalued outstanding loan at a real rate, which may be negative or positive or may vary with the real rate paid on deposits. The monthly repayment is usually set at a constant real amount sufficient to repay interest and revalued loan over its life. Thus during an inflation the monetary repayment required each year would rise each year by the amount of inflation in the previous year. However, incomes also rise in monetary (if not real) terms during inflations, so the proportion of income taken up by mortgage payments in monetary terms remains constant except when interest rates rise.

As the real value mortgage scheme rephases mortgage repayments, a shift from the present unindexed system would produce a temporary hiatus in building societies' cash flow. Various schemes have been proposed for overcoming this. Some rely on temporary diversion of taxpayer's funds by a State refinancing body. Others rely on attracting more funds into the building societies by higher real interest rates. Others propose that real value mortgages be introduced gradually in parallel with existing mortgages so that the scheme can be made separately self-financing.

Although many different schemes of indexing mortgages have been proposed, all share one major virtue: they will eliminate the mortgage holder's vested interest in continuing inflation. At present mortgage payers form a coherent and politically influential group who benefit from accelerating inflation and are extremely vulnerable to unanticipated deflation. Indexation would largely insulate them from inflation. It would thereby remove the influence they insidiously and indirectly bear upon the thought processes of politicians and civil servants who determine how vigorously the battle against inflation may be waged

Wages

Another area where indexed contracts are less prevalent than might be expected, given their advantage in removing unnecessary uncertainty, is wage rates. Of course, numerous wage agreements do include provision for automatic increases in response to price increases. Such provisions spread particularly rapidly during Phase III of the last Conservative Government's incomes policy, which specifically endorsed them. And many companies which have not introduced any formal indexation of wages do have an informal understanding that pay will be adjusted from time to time to keep up with price increases.

Nonetheless large numbers of workers are not covered by formal or informal indexation between annual agreements. The most important reason for this is probably the hostility of trades union officials to indexed contracts. Trades union officials are hostile to indexed contracts for the very simple reason (about which they are often amazingly frank) that such contracts would deprive the union of credit for wage increases which are, in fact, attributable solely to inflation of the monetary demand for labour. Moreover, the unions recognise that the uncertainty and fear of erosion of living standards which prevail between unindexed wage bargains are precisely what generate the union cohesion and militancy typical of inflationary periods. Indexation would reduce this source of militancy by guaranteeing that living standards would be maintained during the contract period.

The empirical evidence that increased industrial militancy is the *consequence* of inflation rather than the root *cause* of it is overwhelming. Thus in the UK, since inflation became rampant, militancy has spread to industries where the unions are not traditionally militant and which are still controlled by 'moderates'. It has even spread to industries and professions which have never had strong unions at all. And in Germany, where the inflation was indisputably the result of a monetary expansion,[6] the first signs of industrial militancy only developed after several years of accelerating inflation.

There is clearly a reasonable general case for employers to stand up to trades unions who resist indexation and to insist that future contracts be indexed. Standing up to unions on ordinary disputes about pay or conditions may be costly and will at best produce a *temporary* net benefit to the employer if he succeeds in keeping down the annual wage bill. By contrast, a successful stand on the issue of indexation promises a *permanent* benefit to the employer (the subsequent reduction of union prestige and militancy)—which is why unions oppose it. Moreover, the chances of a successful stand are reasonably favourable since the interests of employers and employees happen to coincide and to be opposed only to the self-interest of trades union officials.

Obviously indexation would not wholly eliminate the uncertainty which generates industrial militancy. Even if money wages were adjusted monthly to take full account of the preceding month's inflation there would still be some erosion of purchasing power in the interim. More important, the individual has only a confused appreciation of the rate at which prices are rising overall. The retail price index may show that prices have risen by a certain amount which is fully reflected in his pay packet. But he may still feel that prices have risen more or less rapidly than this. Indeed, he may be correct to feel this if his purchases over the period have not been typical of the index. Consequently, so long as inflation remains rapid, quite a number of people at any moment will probably feel that their living standards are being eroded even though, overall, they are protected by indexation.

A major source of theoretical dispute is the nature of the index which should be used in wage settlements. The lay presumption is that the index of consumer prices is appropriate. However, there is a theoretical case for saying that the index should only reflect the domestic component of prices, excluding the impact of import prices or indirect taxes. This is because any change in the terms of trade (e.g. as a result of an increase in the real cost of crude oil) or increase in indirect taxes must result, sooner or later, in a decline in real disposable income in the UK relative to what it would otherwise have been.

If wages were all indexed to the retail price index the process of adjustment to any changes in the terms of trade would be delayed until the next round of wage bargains. On the other hand, if wages were indexed only to an index of the domestic pre-tax component of consumer prices the adjustment would begin immediately a change in the terms of trade or of indirect tax rates occurred. The latter is obviously more desirable.

However, the distinction is fairly theoretical. Most British wage bargains have not been indexed to the retail price or any other index. Yet the temporary decline in real wages produced by a deterioration in the terms of trade which fed through to the price index in 1973–4 was subsequently reversed at the next round of wage settlements. The necessary decline in real living standards was postponed not because of an inappropriate index but because the state of the labour market temporarily permitted successful restoration of real living standards. So it is more important to make sure that demand conditions do not cause indefinite postponement of a necessary drop in the standard of living than to worry that an inappropriate index may delay it by at most a few months.

Discussion of indexation of wages has recently centred on the concept of an indexed wage freeze. This is a highly specific proposal (albeit with variants) to prohibit collective bargaining for a period during which the present pattern of wage rates would be frozen in real terms. Whether or not it is desirable, an indexed wage freeze is quite distinct from the voluntary indexation of specific wage settlements arrived at by free collective bargaining.

Unfortunately, many people who reject the concept of an indexed wage freeze have condemned voluntary indexation by (mis)association. Many of those who object to an indexed wage freeze do so because they recognise the need for a drop in real incomes at times when it is necessary for British workers to price themselves back into full employment. However, voluntary indexation is not synonymous with a permanent guarantee of real incomes or with a State-directed incomes policy. Voluntary indexation merely involves people expressing wage contracts in real terms. Wage bargainers can negotiate lower real wages and express these in indexed terms for the duration of a contract.[7]

Another way in which indexation would affect wage bargaining is through indexation of the tax system. At present unions and workers are well aware that a wage increase sufficient to protect their gross incomes against the expected level of inflation will still leave them worse off after tax. For example, a worker who is at the tax threshold and believes that prices are rising at 20 per cent per annum knows that, with a 35 per cent marginal tax rate, he needs a 31 per cent increase in gross income to maintain his net disposable income. Of course, in performing this sort of calculation he is tacitly assuming that tax thresholds will not be adjusted upwards in line with inflation. In fact, thresholds have been adjusted upwards from time to time—although recently not by enough to prevent an increasing tax burden falling on the lower paid. If employees were assured in advance by indexation of the tax system that tax thresholds would rise in line with inflation, they would recognise that they could maintain both gross and net incomes with a 20 per cent wage increase. This would presumably help to reduce the aggravation of wage-push pressure by inflation.

THE GOVERNMENT'S ROLE

Given that indexation is in general desirable and certainly not harmful if it is accompanied by a disinflationary policy, there is still room for debate as to how far Government should encourage it.

At a minimum the Government might limit itself to indexing its own transactions. Or it might in addition seek to remove the legal, fiscal and institutional obstacles to indexation in the private sector. Finally, it could actually require private firms and individuals to index all suitable types of contract.

Even the 'minimalist' position of indexing Government transactions affords considerable scope for reform, particularly in the spheres of taxation, official borrowing and expenditure.

Most governments are, however, somewhat reluctant to index their own transactions. This is partly because they are the principal beneficiaries of unindexed inflation. There are three ways in which unindexed inflation makes life easier for Governments.

First, as explained above, a Government can resort to inflationary finance to produce and take credit for a short-term pre-election boom: the price inflation and slump which must inevitably follow an artificial boom may not materialise until after the election and can then be blamed on contemporary factors.[8] Indexation would diminish the scope for this manoeuvre since it reduces the impact of expanding demand on output and accelerates its feed through to prices.

Second, governments benefit from the automatic increase in tax revenues which results from 'fiscal drag'. Fiscal drag is the automatic consequence of inflation under a progressive tax system (i.e. a tax system which takes a larger proportion of income the higher the income). As incomes in money terms rise, more and more people move into higher tax brackets. Consequently Government takes a larger share of their incomes—even though the real purchasing power of their incomes may not have increased at all. Fiscal drag enables Governments to take credit for increased public spending without incurring the odium of legislating higher tax rates. Alternatively, Ministers can claim to be generously cutting tax rates while, in fact, taking at least as large a share of people's real incomes as ever.[9]

If tax schedules were linked to the price index Government would only be able to take a larger share of incomes by openly asking Parliament to legislate for a higher real rate of tax.

For example, in the Budget of March 1971 the Chancellor claimed to be cutting taxes to the tune of £184 million. In fact, however, despite knocking off 6*d* from the standard rate of income tax and increasing children's allowances, the total income tax take increased by £840 million or 14 per cent, whereas the increase in the cost of living was only 9 per cent. Similarly, in the March 1975 Budget the Chancellor proudly raised the single and married persons' allowances by 8 per cent and 10 per cent respectively. However, prices in 1975/76 averaged some 25 per cent more than in 1974/75. So the real value of those allowances, in fact, declined by over 11 per cent. Had the basic tax schedules been denominated not in money but in indexed form the Chancellor would have had to ask Parliament to *reduce* the real value of allowances unless he was prepared to forgo the revenue.

What would happen under an indexed tax system is this: the Finance Act would set the value of allowances (and all higher tax thresholds) at a basic money level multiplied by the ratio of the price index at the start of each new period to the index at the base date. Thus if the initial personal allowance had been set at £625 from 1 April 1974 it would automatically have been increased to £757 a year later because the price index rose 21 per cent in that period. Mr Healey would in April 1975 have had to ask Parliament to reduce it almost immediately to £675—the level to which he, in fact, purported to 'raise' it. Possibly, faced with incurring the odium of visibly taxing the poor, he would have endeavoured to forgo some revenue and cut back expenditure by that amount.

In short, the introduction of indexation in Government taxation schedules need not alter the amount and distribution of the tax burden. It would merely force Governments to be open about any increases in the real level of tax which they choose to levy.

It is significant that when some opposition backbenchers proposed an amendment to the 1975 Finance Bill to index tax schedules the Government rejected it on the grounds that it would 'cost' £800 million. What they meant was that they would be forced to reveal to the public that, merely as a result of fiscal drag, and with no change in the tax rates, an extra £800 million was being surreptitiously extracted from the taxpayer's pocket. It might be that the public would welcome the fact that such extra sums are being taken from them and spent for them even if the process was no longer concealed by the veil of money illusion. But the Government clearly doubts it.

The third way in which inflation results in unlegislated increases in tax revenue is capital gains and corporation tax. Increases in capital values which merely reflect inflation are taxed in the same way as genuine increases in real terms. Moreover, since depreciation and stocks are valued on the basis of historic cost rather than current replacement value, the profits on which corporation tax is assessed are overstated. The Chancellor has recently been forced to make an *ad hoc* allowance for artificial stock profits due to inflationary cost increases. The capital gains and replacement cost effect could be largely corrected by adjusting both items by appropriate price indices before calculating tax liability. Most systems of inflation accounting incorporate such adjustments and thereby remove this element of artificial profits. However, the Inland Revenue continues to levy taxes on a historic accounting basis. This in turn has discouraged most companies from presenting their accounts on an inflation-adjusted basis. It is to be hoped that the Sandilands Commission will generate a consensus on a system of inflation accounting suitable both for the presentation of information to shareholders and for the levying of taxes.

The final source of benefit to the Government from unindexed inflation is the reduction in the cost of servicing its borrowing. The Government, including local government, is by far the largest borrower in the country. Most of its debt was issued at fixed interest rates which did not allow for the rate of price inflation which Governments have subsequently permitted to appear. At a rough estimate inflation has lightened the cost of servicing the debt by £10,000 million in 1975/6. This is the extra amount that would have had to be paid had the original long-term debt been indexed and the subsequent inflationary policies been pursued.

If all existing holders of long-term Government securities were now allowed to exchange them for indexed securities of identical term and identical current yield in real terms the total cost of servicing the national debt need not increase one penny. Thus suppose the yield on Government fixed-rate bonds is currently 10 per cent. This may be deemed to be made up of the expected rate of inflation over the life of the bond (say, 8 per cent per annum) and the real rate of interest (by implication 2 per cent). A rational investor will therefore be willing to trade in this bond for an indexed bond with an interest rate of 2 per cent (rising annually with the rate of inflation (as in Table 2.1 above) which will be repayed in constant purchasing-power terms. Indeed, he would probably accept an interest rate significantly below 2 per cent as ample reward for the security of the purchasing-power guarantee. Thus the Government could *reduce* the cost of servicing its borrowing by giving people the opportunity to exchange their existing securities for a similar indexed bond of slightly lower current yield. If the Government then pursues disinflationary policies which succeed in reducing the rate of price inflation, the money cost of servicing their index-linked debt will decline—although the real cost will by definition remain the same. By contrast, if the national debt is left unindexed and the Government brings down the rate of inflation, the real cost of servicing it will be *increased*. This is possibly one reason why Governments with a large *unindexed* national and local debt are not enthusiastic about deflating. Presumably one reason Governments have not indexed their debt is because they wished to retain the option to reduce the debt burden by accelerating the depreciation of the currency.

Servicing debt is no peripheral part of Government expenditure since, despite past depreciation, the national debt currently absorbs about a tenth of Government tax revenues. Indeed, half of the £106 billion public sector borrowing requirement is absorbed by the cost of servicing the public sector.

Of course, Government officials do not usually cite as their reason for rejecting indexation the desirability of retaining the option to depreciate the real cost of servicing the national debt. They usually argue that indexation would 'kill the gilt-edge market' and make it impossible to borrow in the future. They fear that, since indexed securities would be more attractive than unindexed securities, all dealing in existing bonds would cease. Most practical market men share this fear, since practical men are usually afraid of, and incapable of analysing, any situation which is by its very nature hypothetical. However, neither need have the slightest worry. There is a price for everything. So if indexed bonds are more attractive than unindexed bonds they will settle at a higher price and therefore yield a lower real return. Investors will switch between indexed and unindexed bonds according to their varying and varied appreciation of likely inflation rates just as at present dealers switch between long and short gilts. The gilt-edged market will be *healthier* for the extension of its range of securities.

The only forms of indexed saving introduced by the UK Government so far are non-marketable savings under the Save As You Earn (SAYE) scheme and the Pensioners Bonds. The sums involved are not large in comparison with total borrowing by the State. They are apparently intended not as a first step towards general indexation but to head off such a development by appeasing the more politically visible sufferers from unindexed inflation.

These schemes do offer very full protection to the saver. The value of his principal is revalued to allow for inflation, and the saver is not required to pay tax on this revaluation. The rate of interest is therefore zero in real terms, which is much better than has been achieved on similar savings in recent years. Indeed, at the 25 per cent per annum inflation rate experienced during 1975–6 a standard rate taxpayer saving in an unindexed bond would need to receive a nominal interest rate of 38·5 per cent merely to maintain his capital! That is effectively what is being provided by SAYE and Pensioner Bonds.

The major area of Government where indexation is already at all widespread is in its own expenditures. The budgets of all Government departments are set not in terms of cash but in so-called 'real' terms. In fact, however, departments are not, as might be supposed, allowed to set their budget in terms of the previous year's total spending (plus or minus some real increase) grossed up by some general index of prices. Instead they are allowed to calculate the cost of any resources used in the current year at the prices which actually prevailed in the previous year. Thus they have no incentive to economise on the use of those resources which have become relatively scarcer (i.e. whose cost has risen faster than average). Nor do they suffer any penalty if they pay staff at rates higher than are required to recruit an adequate number. It would be far better to establish budgets for each department in terms of cash which could be increased in proportion to the increase in the general price index. This should be the meaning of the much heralded, but so far little practised, cash limits.

Apart from internal budgeting, the only major example of indexation of Government expenditure is in social security payments. Governments have openly promised to increase certain social security benefits, notably pensions, in line with the cost of living. At present the inflation adjustment is made at intervals of up to a year, which means that the real purchasing power of pensions can decline considerably between adjustments. The Conservative Party promised at the 1974 election to adjust twice yearly, which would obviously be more desirable from the pensioner's point of view, though more expensive for the taxpayers.

CONCLUSION

Indexation is the natural response of a market economy to the destruction by inflation of money as a standard of value over time. Whether or not indexation is desirable is secondary: the primary fact is that once inflation is endemic indexation of some kind is inevitable. When, as in Germany in 1923, hyperinflation is reached, virtually every intertemporal transaction has to be frequently adjusted to some standard of reasonably constant purchasing power—be it gold, the dollar or the price index.

Naturally Government can either impede or facilitate the adoption and implementation of indexation. It can remove artificial impediments, provide objective price indices and even make indexation of contracts obligatory. Alternatively, it may forbid or discourage use of indexation.

Of itself indexation is neither a cause of nor a cure for inflation. Its impact will depend on whether the underlying financial forces are inflationary or deflationary. If they are inflationary indexation will speed up the process by which they work through to price rises. Any government which is unwilling or unable to refrain from resorting to inflationary finance will want to suppress the symptoms of that process in order to reap the benefits. So it is most unlikely to encourage indexation. By contrast, indexing can reduce the painful side effects of a deflationary policy and expedite its effect in slowing down price increases. Official encouragement of widespread indexation is therefore appropriate to help, and should be a symptom of determination to overcome, inflation.

Above all a Government determined to overcome inflation (however gradually) should introduce indexation into its own transactions—taxation, budgeting and debt. Inflation will then no longer make life easier for Governments. Instead they will be forced to make honest and open choices about the level of taxation and cost of borrowing. Indexation will help the legislature and electorate to pierce the obfuscation and dishonesty which otherwise characterise inflation.

NOTES AND REFERENCES

1. See the Appendix by Brian Griffiths to Milton Friedman's 'Monetary Correction', Occasional Paper No. 41 of the Institute of Economic Affairs (London, 1974).
2. Which may be consistent with a high but not accelerating rate of inflation.
3. It would usually be better advised to cut its own expenditure, but that is another matter and would merely complicate our explanation.
4. Unless it is that theoretical concept beloved of economists 'perfectly anticipated inflation'—in which case indexation would be unnecessary, since the future inflation rate can be perfectly discounted in the monetary terms of the contract.
5. I should be in favour of indexation even if monetary and fiscal policy were not disinflationary but simply designed to prevent an acceleration of inflation. As there is rarely a medium-term overall financial strategy, and decisions are taken incrementally on a short-term basis, it is necessary to ask in a fairly straightforward way whether moves towards indexation should be welcomed in the UK at present. My answer would be a forthright 'Yes'. S.B.
6. The German money supply increased dramatically in the period 1966–8. This generated the boom of 1968–70 and the consequent acceleration of wages and prices. The initial increase in the money supply was not deliberate but resulted from the inflow of funds into Germany from abroad attracted by a domestic currency which was undervalued.
7. The delays imposed by union power and other obstacles to such reduction are considerable. But there is no evidence that the absence of indexation after 1974 directly made these obstacles worse.
8. Of course, politicians and civil servants do not normally think in these cynical terms. They seem conveniently able to delude themselves time and again that the boom will not be short term but will generate self-sustaining long-term growth. And the possibility of a resurgence of wage and price inflation is dismissed with a touching faith

in the efficiency of price and wage controls. However, such self-delusion has never (with the possible exception of the Heath administration) blinded policy makers to the need to co-ordinate these altruistic policies with the political calendar.

9. Recently there have been suggestions that at our present rapid rates of inflation 'fiscal drag' has been reversed and replaced by 'negative fiscal drag'. However, no one doubts that fiscal drag continues to operate in the personal income tax system. It is simply that revenues from some indirect taxes do not automatically increase with inflation and others only rise *pari passu*, whereas Government expenditures (being wage intensive) may run ahead of prices. Thus even in present circumstances inflation is extracting an increasing proportion of real incomes without legislative assent and redistributing it to public employees and consumers of goods subject to declining indirect taxes.

CHAPTER 3

Controlling Labour Costs in Times of Inflation

E. J. Robertson and R. H. Gilbert

In July 1975 the British Government introduced a £6 limit on pay increases in an effort to contain inflation. It was the sixth time since the war that action of this kind had been taken, and at the outset of this chapter we attempt to set the background which prepared the way for the introduction of the policy. There follows a more general analysis of why Governments find income policies attractive but have difficulties with their timing; some comments are then made on the broader implications for employers arising out of the recurrent adoption of pay controls. Finally, specific advice is given for businessmen on the actions which they should take within their own companies during periods of high inflation to ensure that their views are heard, that problems arising are dealt with at appropriate levels, that labour costs are effectively managed, particularly during the present restraint, and that appropriate information is disclosed to employees in a useful manner.

BACKGROUND TO THE £6 POLICY

Inflation in Britain, which in 1974 had been higher than in most other advanced industrial countries, worsened during 1975 at a time when the inflation rates elsewhere were falling. British industry's unit costs were moving increasingly out of line, undermining the competitive position of British goods and placing greater pressure on sterling.

Below capacity working increased among firms in manufacturing industry. Furthermore, companies were facing falling demand while their costs continued to escalate and their liquidity situation remained difficult. The prospect was one of a low level of capital spending by industry and of a sharp fall in manufacturing employment.

It was clear that if this situation continued there would be further rises in unemployment, already worse than at any time since the 1930s. Britain's industrial base was being weakened by bankruptcies and contraction as companies became increasingly unable to compete in world markets, whilst resultant damage to its foreign loan capacity was particularly hampering to a nation reliant on the import of many raw materials and with the status of an international finance and banking centre. There was increasing recognition that the solution to Britain's inflation lay principally in Britain itself. For a short period up to about the middle of 1974 the main cost pressure had come from increased import prices beyond UK control, and competitors had suffered similarly; pay settlements which implied continuing acceptability of high inflation had grown, and the grave dangers attendant upon this had been ignored. Thus the proportion of total cost increases in the UK directly attributable to labour cost increases rose drastically, as was indicated in the reports of the Price Commission. The proportion, which stood at 15 per cent in March to May 1974 and at 24 per cent in June to August 1974, had gone up to 33 per cent by September to November 1974 and was continuing at that level. Furthermore, as the Price Commission emphasised, this underestimated the real impact of rising labour costs:

> To a large extent increased material costs reflect increased labour costs incurred by the supplier. This is particularly important in the case of industries such as engineering which rely heavily on bought in components. If this factor is taken into account, we estimate that, in the three months to November increased labour costs would have accounted not for 33 per cent of price increases, but 60 per cent . . . There is no question whatever about the steep upward trend of unit labour costs and the pressure on prices that this is exerting . . . The future depends therefore first and foremost on trend of labour costs. So long as the present spate of labour cost increases continue the prospects are bleak.[1]

To these growing pressures must be added the particular political embarrassment faced by a Labour Government. In addition to the action to halt the spread of unemployment which was increasingly expected of the Government by its traditional supporters, there was the real prospect that funds for public expenditure would not be available since wealth was not being created by industry and since money could not be borrowed; the maintenance of welfare provisions at existing levels might prove impossible, whilst their extension to cover new areas of deprivation could not be contemplated, and finance for further Socialist measures would not be available.

Finally, the Opposition, the employers and the unions themselves agreed that the pay restraint of the Government's Social Contract with the TUC had failed: external creditors pressed increasingly for stronger action.

THE LASTING ATTRACTION OF INCOMES POLICY

All these factors contributed to the decision by the Labour Government—more strongly and publicly opposed than any of its predecessors to intervention in wage determination—to adopt an incomes policy. It was not, however, the first Government in recent times to change its view on the role of incomes policy as an economic regulator. In the years since 1966 a Labour Government using the law to limit the level of pay settlements in the face of Conservative opposition had been followed by a Conservative Government imposing wage controls in the face of Labour opposition. These continuing changes of view and policy create two areas of difficulty for businessmen.

First, of the fact that the parties traditionally associated with labour and capital have both failed to adopt a conclusive policy towards intervention by law in the determination of pay is confusing. Respectable spokesmen in either party can be found to make the case for or against incomes policy; some can be found in prominent positions who have done both. This makes it difficult for those actually engaged in managing business to identify with a particular view.

Second, an incomes policy makes business planning more uncertain. The imposition of the policy (or belief in its imminence) affects settlement levels, recruitment and retention, a fact which we will examine in some detail when we come to look at the practical considerations arising from the £6 policy. For example, no sensible company will wish to find itself unable to offer similar rates to those paid by competitors for key employees, and many may think twice about shedding labour if an incomes policy is imminent which will make future recruitment more difficult Furthermore, in the past an incomes policy has not come alone but, as in the case of the Conservative policy of 1972–4, has been accompanied by a paraphernalia of controls in other fields, notably prices and dividends. Whether an incomes policy is about to be introduced or not is thus of considerable importance to effective company management.

Advantages and Disadvantages

The primary attraction to Governments of incomes policy is that it promises, according to some analysts (*see* Chapter 1), to offer control over inflation, whilst avoiding the unpleasant choices offered by severe demand management or monetary policies.

Labour costs have been shown repeatedly to be the main element of inflationary pressure in the British economy. Although other items—such as national insurance contributions, State and company pension costs, overtime payments and shift premia—can be costly to employers, basic pay naturally remains the largest determinant of labour costs. The remainder, for example rises in the price of insurance stamps, are mostly under direct Government control, but the pre-eminence of unrestricted collective bargaining in a local and national form in this country has meant that pay determination is largely outside the area of direct Government influence. The argument runs that if pay is controlled labour costs can be contained and the major inflationary engine will be halted.

Because inflation is a problem which has been foremost in British politics since the war—notwithstanding the thorny question of our relationship with the European Community—no Government can afford to exclude finally from its policy options anything that may help reduce it. Statutory incomes control, however, has not been the first choice of policy instrument for Governments at the commencement of a term of office, for several reasons.

Firstly, since an incomes policy is designed to reduce the level of pay settlements below what they would have been in its absence, a promise of its introduction is effectively a promise to people that they will receive less pay than they would otherwise do. This does not make it the strongest of planks on which to build an electoral platform. On no occasion has a Government been elected which included in its manifesto a pledge to introduce statutory control of incomes. The 1974 Conservative Government was refused a mandate on such a policy; its own conversion to legal control of pay increases had in any event come two years into its period of office. But long before that, the 1948 'freeze' on incomes was introduced in the third year of the Attlee Government; the 1961–2 'Pay Pause' followed two years after a general election; the pay standstill of August 1966 and the statutory controls thereafter were not mentioned in the Labour Manifesto in March of that year; and the current controls represent a Government *volte face* sixteen months after taking office.

Secondly, commitment to an incomes policy carries with it the opposition of vested interests. Those whose livelihood (and indeed power) depends upon the negotiation of higher pay are unlikely to welcome legal restraint on their activities. When the vested interest is as strong as our contemporary trades union movement, this is a very substantial disincentive. Fierce opposition from this quarter at the outset of any Government's period of office can make implementation of policies in many areas difficult; further, the power of the trades unions to disrupt normal life in pursuit of pay settlements beyond prescribed limits can undermine public support generally for a Government.

Thirdly, when political parties adopt statutory control of incomes as a policy they are often seen by opponents and commentators as ruling out other policy options based on different theories of the causes of inflation. Politicians are thus reluctant to commit themselves to an incomes policy and thereby to state on which ground they will stand when there is a perfectly convenient fence on which to sit—namely, 'keeping their options open'—or a vote-winning alternative in the shape of opposition to pay controls.

Finally, political leaders have become increasingly sensitive to charges of pragmatism and of government by U-turns. One effect of this has been to find new combinations of words to hide policy changes—thus the 1975 pay legislation is concealed behind the title 'Remuneration Charges and

Grants Act'. Another effect perhaps has been to slow down the rate of change of attitude towards various policies, if not to stop it altogether. When a subject is of such prominent interest and public sensitivity as incomes policy, it is difficult for parties and personalities not to adopt views on it: for those committed during an election to an adverse view, in order to avoid alienating support, the possibility of a 'quick change' once in Government to meet new circumstances may be accordingly reduced.

Although for these reasons it is not easy for a Government to embark on policies of incomes restraint early in its term of office, experience indicates that it can be equally hazardous to adopt pay controls later in a five-year term. Governments have sought either to reduce the level of pay settlements by allowing little increase in incomes or none at all (the 'freeze' approach) or to endeavour to bring the level down by gradual stages (the 'n–1' approach). Given high initial levels of inflation, either approach is now, however, widely recognised to mean control of pay increases over a period of years. Thus, if the 'freeze' approach is adopted, the problem immediately arises of how to get out of it: it cannot be maintained indefinitely, but if it is lifted quickly, pay settlements can be expected to continue as they did before, or even at a higher level as compensation is sought for the period of restraint. Moreover, the very nature of the 'n–1' approach will reduce pay settlements by steps and, therefore, to have any effect must be kept for more than one year. Once an incomes policy has been adopted, a Government must expect to be able to keep it on for a number of years if it is to be effective. There must be either progressively more generous settlements from a low base or progressively less generous pay settlements from a high base until price increases and pay increases have both reached acceptable competitive levels.

A party which in government successfully overcame the problems associated with incomes policy and thereby succeeded in stopping or greatly reducing rises in prices could expect the fulsome gratitude of the electorate at the next and succeeding elections. The prospect, then, of a long period of uninterrupted power with the means available for putting into practice the party's ideas beckons strongly. If there is a poll before the conclusion of the policy, however, the same Government can expect to reap a more bitter electoral harvest. Those who have followed the restraint on pay but have not yet received a return in the benefits deriving from reduced inflation may suspect or know that others have been less faithful in their observance. In any event, they are likely to find attractive the opportunity for negotiating more pay and for abandoning the difficulties caused by legal restraint. A Government which introduces an incomes policy when it has less than three or four years to run will be risking the second outcome and thus removal from power. Catch 22 in fact.

The Alternatives

The severe difficulties for a Government in introducing an incomes policy early in its period of office, and the dangers associated with imposition of statutory controls towards the end of its life, would suggest that other possible solutions based on different assessments of the causes of inflation might prove more attractive. The alternatives, however, have their own disadvantages in terms of parliamentary timetables and public acceptability.

The first—tight control of the money supply—is believed to produce very high levels of unemployment. Since the experience of the 1930s, and in view of the social consequences, politicians are reluctant to be associated with a policy which is seen as throwing people out of work. Furthermore, the direct costs of increasing unemployment are considerable. In addition to the waste of manpower, the rise in the level of unemployment pay and social security benefits would be a considerable charge on the State, entailing greater sacrifices by those remaining in work; and the cost of redundancies in the interim could prove a crushing burden even to viable companies.

The second alternative—use of fiscal controls—is also believed to produce more unemployed and thereby shares the disadvantage of pure monetarist policy. Its effectiveness is likely to be reduced in any case by two developments. Firstly, the growth of threshold and other index-linked payments has reduced the ability of Government to manage demand through indirect taxation.[2] Secondly, some unions—notably in white collar areas—are showing an increasing tendency to take account of any rises in income tax in negotiating subsequent pay settlements, thereby negating the Chancellor's intentions and restricting his capacity to use direct taxation as a tool of demand management.

Although it can be seen that all policy options carry with them attendant political disadvantages, repeated experiences of the kind undergone during 1974–5 indicate that Governments cannot permit themselves the luxury of ignoring the problems of inflation. Domestically, inflation leads to uncertainty and insecurity for investors, for companies in their accounting and planning, and for the public at large. It tends to rule by jungle law: those with the strongest bargaining power increase their pay to anticipate inflation, whilst the weak, the disorganised, and others on low and fixed incomes have their incomes and their ability to purchase the necessities of life reduced. Inflation also saps confidence internationally, and a country which borrows money abroad to the extent that Britain does cannot ignore the views of its creditors.

IMPLICATIONS FOR BUSINESSMEN

We have sought to put across the view that inflation is a problem which Governments cannot ignore; that they must take account of all courses open to them which may help reduce inflation; and that these courses include attempts to limit labour costs by statutory control of pay rises.

There are four broad implications resulting from this analysis which, we suggest, require close study by businessmen and managers.

- Businessmen should seek a full understanding of the inflationary process, of the theories of inflation and of the various possible policies open to Governments in attempts to reduce inflation.
- In particular, they should endeavour to develop a view on the role of incomes policy.
- In the best interests of their company and industrial relations, they should be aware of the times when it is most likely that Governments will resort to limiting pay rises.
- They should ensure that their views are heard—both before the introduction of any pay limits and during their operation—through employers' organisations and contacts with Government officials at local and national level.

The last of these points we cover in detail in a later section dealing with practical advice to businessmen. The others, however, deserve fuller attention here.

Achieving an Understanding of the Inflationary Process

The first conclusion implies a study of inflation, at least covering the period since the war, and of the various theories of its causation with their accompanying patent cures. An excellent summary is given by Professor Prest in Chapter 1, and there is much published literature on the subject.

The Role of Incomes Policy

There is also a wide variety of reading material on the use of incomes control.[3] Companies should draw their own conclusions by studying internal experience during periods of pay policy, at least in the most recent period (November 1972–July 1974). Indicators for assessing the effects include labour costs—the relationship between increases agreed and statutory limits; industrial relations—days lost through disputes and the number whose main cause was pay; narrowing of differentials—the effects of ceilings and preferential limits for the lower paid on executive recruitment and retention, on wage and salary structures, and on disputes over differentials; productivity changes and manning levels; threshold agreements—the use, consolidation and cost of any indexation or payments in lieu; and fringe benefits—the attention paid in negotiation to improvements in terms and conditions outside pay. Account should also be taken of the effects of the price and dividend restraints accompanying pay control.

Precursors of Intervention on Pay

Whatever view businessmen adopt towards inflation and its control, advice on spotting the omens which presage intervention by Government on pay must inevitably be tentative. There have been only two occasions when a full-blown statutory policy has been introduced (1966–70 and 1972–4): to derive general laws from such limited sources would clearly be absurd. Nevertheless it is possible to point to some indicators on the following lines: when inflation is likely to become a cause of sufficient concern to a Government to warrant the implementation of strong measures —fiscal, monetary or the control of incomes—with the attendant electoral risks; when attention will be directed towards labour costs and interest in incomes policy increases; when the disadvantages of adopting an incomes policy will be minimised and the advantages maximised; and the actions likely to be taken by Government immediately before presenting an incomes policy.

There is no single fixed figure below which rises in prices can be tolerated and above which they require remedy. Action in the shape of an incomes policy was taken in 1972 when inflation was running at 7·6 per cent per annum, but the statutory controls were lifted in July 1974 when the rate of increase in prices was 17·1 per cent per annum. The 'Attack on Inflation' White Paper heralding the latest effort was introduced when the annual rate was 26·3 per cent. Concern is related to a wide number of circumstances, which include:

- when the rate of increase in prices is high and accelerating from month to month;
- when it is higher than in other countries with which Britain competes;
- when the trade deficit is increasing and British goods are becoming less competitive abroad;
- when the pound is falling in relation to other currencies;
- when credit from abroad is required and proves difficult to obtain or is being foreclosed on.

Interest is more likely to rise in the use of incomes policy as an instrument to limit inflation in a situation characterised by:

- pay settlements being concluded at levels above the rise in prices;
- productivity not increasing at a rate likely to compensate for the rise in pay in excess of the rise in prices;
- unit labour costs increasing at a rate in excess of those in competing countries;

- the rise in prices being attributable to rises in pay.

The disadvantage to politicians and Governments of adopting incomes control as a policy will be least at times:

- when a general election is not imminent;
- when a reasonable period has passed after any general election during which the winning party was opposed to Government interference in pay determination;
- when the wage round is drawing to a close or is just commencing;
- when those with vested interests in Government intervention, in particular the trades unions and to a lesser extent employers' organisations, are not implacably opposed to the Government or to incomes policy;
- when there is widespread public support for control of pay.

Immediate 'run-up' periods to the introduction of Government intervention on pay have shown the following characteristics:

- the 'exhaustion' of alternative options, i.e. when further pursuit of fiscal and monetary policy is believed to cause unacceptable levels of unemployment;
- sonorous warnings from Government Ministers, authoritative bodies such as the National Institute and representatives of foreign creditors about the level of pay settlements;
- tripartite talks between the Government, the TUC and the CBI, together or separately aimed at producing an effective policy on voluntary grounds;
- insufficient agreement within the talks to avoid a worsening of the situation.

It must be stressed that the lists of circumstances outlined above as producing a climate in which Government interference in pay determination is likely are not intended to be exhaustive; they are neither necessary nor sufficient conditions for pay policies. Wage limitation may be introduced when the situation is less catastrophic; other events may occur before action on pay is taken; or action via different routes may be used.

They are, however, suggested as helpful guidelines. Many of the conditions applied when the Labour Government took action in July 1975. As was noted earlier, prices were high and had been accelerating,[4] whilst those in competing countries were falling; the pound was depreciating; although there was some indication of improvement in balance of trade, prices of British goods were becoming less competitive; and foreign creditors were pressing for action. Pay rises continued to be at levels ahead of price increases, and both were running far in excess of possible improvements in productivity; whilst pay in Britain was lower than in other advanced countries, our labour costs were increasing out of line with our competitors';[5] and price increases were increasingly being attributed to pay rises. Furthermore, the Government was reasonably established and a general election seemed some years away; the year of the 'Social Contract' and the wage round associated with it had almost been concluded; the trade unions were proving amenable following the passage into law of much of the agreed Labour Party/TUC programme, whilst the employers were calling for an effective pay policy. Public support for a statutory policy, as reflected in opinion polls, was high. Talks with the TUC and the CBI had taken place in the light of critical comment from economic analysts and international financiers.

THE NEW ANTI-INFLATION POLICY

A fuller account of what the terms of the £6 policy mean for employers in pay negotiations is given later, but we wish to highlight here two important points concerning the 1975 proposals which significantly differentiate them from previous pay policies, and of which employers should be aware.

Firstly, contrary to biblical precedent, the White Paper makes it more damnable to give than to receive: the pay limits are enforceable only on employers. It has been made quite clear that, whilst stronger legal powers have been held in reserve should the policy show signs of failure, there will be no question of bringing unions or employees who seek and receive increases above the limits into a court of law for their activities.

Secondly, and related to the first point, the policy has changed the emphasis on the benefits which may be received as a result of obeying the limit from the achievement of lower prices to the avoidance of mass unemployment. In addition, as is explained below, in facing practical aspects of the policy, the mechanisms of enforcement may well mean that the threat of unemployment will be one which directly affects the employee claiming a pay reward in excess of the limit.

The threat of seeing those they represent thrown out of work should they break the pay limit may prove to be a stronger incentive to negotiators to hold to the policy than the rather abstract achievement of lower price rises for the population as a whole has been in the past. But it places employers in an invidious position should pressures develop to exceed the ceiling. They can easily be cast as scapegoats if the policy fails. If inflation occurs at a rate higher than that compatible with the £6 policy, industry may well be blamed for paying excessively and 'hiding' settlements which have broken the limit. If unemployment continues to grow despite the pay policy, this may be attributed to employers who broke the limit and who, unable to adjust their prices to reflect big labour cost increases, offset the loss from them by causing redundancies.

These have not been features of previous pay policies, and if businessmen do not wish them to remain part of the current policy they must prepare their arguments for the discussions which will precede the next stage of the policy. For there will be a second stage. The present policy is of the 'n–1' variety: in other words, at least one more year with a new, lower pay target can be expected, starting in August 1976. This is reflected in the provisions for renewal of powers contained in the Remuneration Charges and Grants Act 1975.

PRACTICAL MOVES IN TIMES OF INFLATION

We now wish to concentrate the attention of employers and businessmen on action. Most people engaged in entrepreneurial or executive activity in business and commerce are so engaged because they have a taste and inclination for the practical; certainly they are used to exercising thought on the selection of options and the weighing up of balance of advantage. But they do so because they wish to act; businessmen are judged on results, and results flow from action.

It appears to us that the actions that businessmen might take in regard to labour matters in times of inflation fall into the following categories:

- Ensuring that their individual and representational views about Government policies in the field are coherently expounded and intelligently presented to Government and its various agencies.
- Ensuring that employment policy in general and collective bargaining policy in particular are given an important allocation of time and energy by the chairman, managing director and senior executives.
- Ensuring that labour costs are kept under the closest scrutiny, and that every imaginative approach to the stabilisation of these costs in an inflationary climate is examined on its merits. These actions are particularly important in periods of incomes policy, and are examined in the light of the current limits.
- Ensuring that the company has a sensible and practical information policy so that it can communicate effectively with its own employees.

We propose to examine each of these categories in more detail.

Influencing Government: The Importance of Making Views Clear

It is hardly surprising that writers with a background of experience in the CBI should return at this point to the importance of businessmen making their views known. Professor Prest in the opening chapter of this text states that:

> In a world where Government decisions are very frequently taken in response to the shrill cries or threatening menaces of pressure groups operating at parliamentary or Civil Service levels business enterprises clearly cannot afford that their voices be unheard in such jamborees.

Although one might quarrel with the choice of the word 'jamboree', the advice is nevertheless very sound. The method chosen by businessmen to influence Government—for example, trying to convince them that price and dividend restraints need not be automatic accompaniments of pay restraint —is to some extent dictated by the size and influence of the company. Large influential companies certainly do go it alone: discreet dinners for Ministers, cocktail parties for MPs, discussion at all levels with the Civil Service, these methods the large companies can and do use. Of course, such representations are extended to a complete range of industrial and commercial matters, and it is right that this is so; a difficulty in the matter of living with inflation—or suggesting ways in which it might be countered —is that this direct access to Government enjoyed by some companies can be counter-productive in a particularly interesting way. To illustrate, suppose we envisage a situation in which Minister X, in the course of a discussion with Industrialist Y on, say, investment prospects, is prompted to observe 'Surely you are not one of those misguided businessmen who fall for the line that business cannot live with free collective bargaining and must rely upon the dubious protection of a statutory incomes policy?' Industrialist Y, probably still thinking of his brief on investment and certainly not wishing to offend a Minister he has come to influence on this different matter, says 'Of course I am not one of those backswoodsmen. Why only the other day I had to remind my personnel man that I had built up this business in a free market economy and who was he to say that it should be interfered with even to the extent of interfering with wage and salary levels. We must be free to bid up for staff we require; if we do not our competitors will.' And so another Cabinet discussion on the need to create an effective incomes policy is subject to Minister X saying, 'Well, only the other day I was talking to Sir —— (and we all know he is no supporter of the Party) and he said that his firm had to remain free to . . .' He goes on to add that the CBI, of which Sir —— is a prominent member, evidently does not represent the views of its members when it asks the Government to do something to restrain wage-led inflation.

Businessmen with the unique advantage of direct access to Whitehall are often used in this way. The answer, of course, is to be well aware, and in full support, of representative policies on major matters such as incomes policies. And refuse to depart from them in discussion with Whitehall—at any level. The trade unions, who currently have enormous influence with Government, know this basic truth of representation very well. They are most difficult to split off—and pretty caustic with anyone who offends in this respect.

Standard advice in this field might be summed up this way:

- Small employers should support an appropriate employers' organisation; and try to see that its views on matters of such major subjects as inflation and inflation control reflect the practical necessities of business as they see them. If this is not so, make a fuss; this policy will probably result in your being appointed to office in the organisation, but then what better way to gain influence?
- Small employers can also do well in getting their views over to the Government if they are listened to at regional level by civil servants of an appropriate department. It seems to us that the Department of Employment is particularly well organised and well informed at that level, and the views of employers thought well of by Regional Controllers in that Department do not languish long in the provinces. They are fed in and often are influential—because they have the merit of apparently being unsought.
- Large employers with frequent direct access to Whitehall should, as we have said, beware of being drawn into giving opinions on matters which may be the subject of central employers' policy. More positively, large companies should take the lead not only in the formation of these policies but also in ensuring that the policies are known to such staff who go off lobbying to other Ministries.
- Chase officials of both employers' organisations and Government; both expect businessmen to behave in such virile ways and are constantly disappointed to find that this is rare. If the chasing is supported by good co-ordinated staff work, so much the better.

The Importance of Employment Policy and Industrial Relations Policy in Inflationary Times

Some general observations should be made about personnel and industrial relations problems in an era of inflation. For example, the difficulties of recruitment, retention, training and so on are magnified considerably, and thus we propose to discuss this aspect separately. In addition, the problems of deciding and operating an industrial relations policy are increased considerably.

Recruitment/training development. It is obvious that in an era of full employment, and in many cases special scarcities of certain types of labour, it is necessary to have some sort of policy for selection and recruitment. It is important to note, however, that in 'stagflation' conditions, where inflation is high, investment slumps and job opportunities fall, some modification of recruitment policy may have to be considered. Many companies operate on the principle that they are in favour of selecting applicants for promotion from inside the company. Thus recruitment may be concentrated principally on school leavers, graduates and the odd replacements for key men. The clearing banks, for example, probably fall into this category. Other companies will take the view that at least a certain proportion of, say, supervisory and management posts must be filled from outside so as to bring new ideas and vitality into the company. Such a view can, of course, be combined with promoting from within when the necessary talent and experience is available. Now if it is accepted that in conditions in which inflation is combined with fewer job opportunities staff wastage will decrease, it seems that a company operating a policy of reserving a fixed proportion of promotion posts for outsiders may find that such a policy will come under increasing pressure. In that case it seems to us right to make a virtue out of necessity and, far from cutting down training and development of staff, companies should try to increase their efforts in this direction. Companies will have an important additional reason for policy change in that the tendency of outsiders to disturb differentials and upset grading schemes becomes much greater in a time of high inflation. There is little doubt that a policy of bringing in a set proportion of outsiders in key positions is a good one. But, like other good things, it must suffer because of inflation. Much of the above comment is, of course, really relevant only to staff recruitment policies. Quite different factors predominate in the selection and recruitment of manual and production workers, factors such as the going rate and capability, and these will be discussed separately under the heading of collective bargaining policies. Certainly with the spread of white collar unions some of these factors become much the same, and these will also be dealt with under the heading of collective bargaining.

Pointers for industrial relations policy. Inflation puts a great strain upon the process of collective bargaining. Structures and institutions which have served well enough in less critical times will be tested severely by high rates of inflation. Thus directors and senior managers will be obliged to take a rather closer look at arrangements for collective bargaining than may have customarily been the case; again, an instance of a useful state of affairs emerging from misfortune. However, the strains of inflation tend very markedly to increase unrest; quite apart from increased militancy on the shop floor, employers have to contend with groups such as clerks supervisors, specialist professionals and middle managers who are all badly hit by inflation and who thus try to protect themselves by attitudes and actions which would be foreign to them in normal circumstances.

In practical terms employers have little alternative but to keep their heads down within the existing framework of industrial relations during periods of inflation. Such periods are not exactly favourable for implementing new initiatives with regard to collective bargaining arrangements. However, by reason of a process of what is almost analogous to testing to destruction, excellent lessons are laid out for the positive and farsighted employer to note so that he can plan for action on collective bargaining arrangements when times are more propitious. For example, a company may find that a policy which allows subsidiaries a free rein on wage and salary levels and trusts to the effect of commercial controls and restraints on the management of the subsidiary companies to keep labour costs at a reasonable level may run into trouble during an inflationary period. The company might thus plan not to centralise bargaining but to set up, when appropriate, a system of central guidelines and monitoring; normally the introduction of such a system, given the independence of companies accustomed to exercising their own judgement in these matters, is difficult. It will, we judge, be much less difficult in a situation where subsidiary directors have been given a severe fright by the effect of parity claims and high inflation.

Again, dispute procedures which may have been adequate in times of gentle inflation can show severe disadvantages in an inflationary situation; similarly arrangements in multi-union situations. The wise employer will note these facts and again plan to improve arrangements when he can. The parallel with other cost factors is obvious; many companies find that a period of prosperity followed by a number of lean years is a time in which valuable lessons, vital to the future success of the company if it survives, are there to be learned.

Our personal opinion is that, despite the fashionability—or perhaps notoriety—of industrial relations and collective bargaining generally, many companies have paid only lip service to putting much stress on, and real top-level influence behind, 'people' policies. They had better take them seriously from now on—if they survive the interval.

Labour Cost Control and the £6 Policy

At the time of writing, businessmen have to contend with a quite specific incomes policy, and so the following observations are directed at helping employers to live with the present policy of statutory price control on them and no pay controls on the unions.

First, let us look at the policy itself. The July 1975 measures are based on the Remuneration Charges and Grants Act 1975. Sections 1 to 3 of that Act, which relate to pay and prices, are linked to three previous components namely:

- The Counter-Inflation Act 1973.[6]
- The Price Code established under Section 2.[7]
- The White Paper 'The Attack on Inflation'.[8]

The legislation gives the Secretary of State for Employment the crucial responsibilities on the pay side. Firstly, he may exempt from liability for breach of contract an employer who refuses to pay his employees sums which have been contractually agreed before the 1975 Act came into effect because such payment could be in excess of the amount laid down by the pay limits.

Secondly, the Secretary of State may issue a negative certificate to the Price Commission which states that in the case of a particular price application the pay limits have been exceeded and therefore the whole of the costs associated with the pay increase are to be disallowed.

The pay limits themselves are based upon the White Paper and upon key statements made by Ministers in the House between 21 and 31 July 1975. We do not intend to detail the limits here, but we will make some points that we consider of importance for industrial relations policy which emerge from the pay limits and the operation of the anti-inflation policy. At present the only guide to the pay limits available is that published by the CBI; this has been published with the approval of the Department of Employment and should be closely studied by employers.

We intend to discuss the following points in connection with the present policy:

- Necessity of adequate comparative information on rates and earnings by district and by trade.
- Distribution of earnings within company.
- Negotiating style and employee/union attitudes.
- Possible changes in payment system policy.
- Productivity.

Comparative rates and earnings. In normal circumstances it is important for companies to know where they stand in relation to those with whom they compete for labour, that is to say for certain broad occupations. Comparisons must be made within the local labour market, and in specialist and key occupations this comparison must extend to the industry (and in some cases to what is paid to such people in the international market). The speed and volatility of wage and salary movements in an inflationary situation means at the very least that salary and wage reviews which are generally carried out at yearly intervals will have to be carried out more frequently, and that a close watch will have to be kept on outside settlements which are considered to be potentially influential in the company. One often finds that such tasks are carried out by comparatively low-level staff—even if senior personnel specialists are involved in the interpretation of the results. However, in an inflationary climate it is advised that high-level input be applied to wage and salary comparisons, and other help may have to be sought.

A number of current publications are useful in this respect, for example

Incomes Data Services and *Industrial Relations Review and Report*; the Department of Employment's *Gazette* should also be studied closely. Companies should note that the larger employers' organisations conduct very detailed wage and salary surveys (the Engineering Employers Federation is outstanding in this respect) and consider using their influence with their own organisation to initiate or improve in this area of activity.

Earnings distribution within the company. Detailed analysis of the distribution of earnings within companies is one of those tasks which are approached on at least three functional levels in companies. Firstly, and obviously, all companies possess the raw data in the shape of payrolls and salary bills; however, it is understandably rare for payroll sections to undertake analyses of this data. Secondly, the raw data may be utilised in preparation for (or response to) collective bargaining situations. Often such analysis is piecemeal and undertaken with a view to responding to, say, a particular parity claim by the unions. Thirdly, the raw data may be analysed for personnel research purposes, for example to try to determine movement in differentials over a period of years, changes in earnings compared to changes in skill mix and so on. This latter analysis is bound to increase in importance in the context of the present incomes policy.

The principal feature of the policy, that is the £6 figure paid as a supplement to earnings and which is not consolidated, can be presumed to lead to erosion of existing differentials over the course of the year 1975–6. Differentials, of course, are important as allocators of labour as well as sources of discontent in pay comparisons, but in a situation where incomes policy tends to reduce differentials it is essential for companies to know where and at what point this process is taking place. One does not need to subscribe to the theory that there must be a differential explosion at the end of a flat-rate incomes policy to be convinced that companies will have to use what limited freedom they might expect in July 1976 to readjust differentials in the interests of efficiency and labour retention. If, *annus mirabilis*, no adjustment of differentials is possible in a Stage II policy, then companies may have to plan for a reallocation of tasks and possible deskilling to accommodate the labour market provisions which will, in a rigid circumstance, certainly build up. No incomes policy—and the present one is not likely to be an exception—can prevent the competitive job movement of people who want to better earnings which they feel have been eroded by diminishing differentials, and in consequence companies may have to combine the odd bit of discreet poaching with fairly radical rethinking about labour requirements and skill mixes. If one assumes that poaching will be self-cancelling, then the rethink may be crucial.

Negotiating style and employee/union attitudes. As Hilda Behrend has so lucidly illustrated,[9] whilst employees may be able to see, understand and even accept the arguments which have been put forward to them by successive Governments (as we have noted, the present incomes policy represents the sixth time since the war that employers have been exposed to Government action on these lines) on the necessity for pay restraint, in their actual behaviour, and more importantly in their behaviour as represented by the actions of unions on their behalf, employees see their own pay demands and perceived needs as purely a reaction to price increases and the pay rises of other people rather than as bringing about price inflation and other people's demands for more pay. In consequence, many employees feel that the only result of pay restraint on their part will be that they will be left behind. To put it another way the concept of pay restraint is not subject to constructive reinforcement.

We take the view, however, that the 1975 policy's crucial link with prices may lead on the other hand to negative reinforcement—which is at least as good as a learning device. In brief, if a company is being pressured—as many may be—to exceed the pay limits, an interesting situation will arise in relation to a possible price increase application. Simply, if the company decides to give in, it will get a negative certificate from the Department of Employment. The Price Commission will be obliged to disallow the entire rise in labour cost resulting from the settlement and the company will be obliged to absorb all the pay costs itself. In many cases that will result in lay-offs as companies try to recoup the labour costs and remain competitive. Thus it will be crucial for companies, in the actual negotiating situation, to get shop stewards in particular to understand this pay–price link mechanism. For the first time, then, an incomes policy incorporates a direct feedback device, namely observe the pay limits or see *your* job security—and not just other people's job security—materially decrease. Clearly the learning process will require a few object lessons, but these should not be too difficult to find in the private sector in the winter of 1975–6. Employers should endeavour to use these object lessons—and not be one themselves.

Changing payment systems. Whilst the sharper arrows of parity and comparability will not be whizzing around in the event of the success of the present anti-inflation policy, the bows which propel them will not be discarded. Thus employers will do well to use the breathing space to examine their present system of payment to see if it can be reformed so as to reduce comparability pressures, when these emerge into the open again. Systems such as job evaluation and measured day work may well have short-term productivity disadvantages compared with bonus and piece work systems, but they offer the possibility of attaining, at least at plant level, an agreed and rational system of wage determination. Planning for such changes in an incomes policy period may be a good long-term investment.

Productivity. Finally, employers will have to face up to the unpalatable fact that, once again, they will be offering more money for at best the same work as last year (and at worst a good deal less). This will be an almost inevitable consequence of the effect of the present policy on innovation and on change. In past incomes policies Governments have tried to build in 'productivity' features at some stage of the policy. This process had particularly bad results in 1967–9, when so-called productivity bargains were used by unions and managements as collusive devices to pay more. In many cases—and indeed on the evidence of increase of movements in prodictivity at a national level, most cases—these bargains resulted in more pay for very little sustained increase in productivity. That this proved to be so was a source of sorrow to one of the present writers, who saw in productivity bargaining the seeds of a very significant advance in the quality of relations at plant level.

No doubt the same pressures will build up on the present policy. One expects, however, that while the Government makes up its mind about productivity exceptions in the next stage of the policy many companies will be driven to improve the unit labour cost position by attempting, in the unpromising circumstances of union opposition and high unemployment, to reduce manning levels. There will certainly be some who will not manage to do this and who may in consequence go under.

Less crude solutions will be sought, at least in planning terms, by companies who are in less dire straits. Commentators' advice on improving productivity is generally more than useless; managers improve productivity by knowing their business and by being good managers; good managers are those who plan for the consent of work forces in advance. Such consent will be vital, and those companies who are fortunate enough to have time available to them during the present policy had better use that time to develop sensible discussions with their work people and their representatives to prepare for positive joint efforts to improve productivity and hence job security. It is in this connection that the final section of this chapter, which deals with information policy, is so important.

The Importance of an Information Policy

It is certain that inflation sharpens the need for companies to tell their employees as much as is practicable about the business in which they work and the economic situation in which it operates. A difficulty is that companies cannot produce and operate an information policy and expect it to have useful results overnight. Indeed, companies will have to face up to the fact that the release of information may very well have results which are initially counterproductive—particularly so in a difficult demand and inflationary situation when they may be accused by employees of only hastening to open the books when there is nothing very much in them. Companies, however, who have made a practice of giving facts to their employees—even simple factual representations of information prepared for the annual report—have found that when inflationary factors cause difficulties for them the employees are infinitely more sensible and understanding in their reaction than would otherwise be the case.

It is in this light that we detail some guidelines for companies (which are adapted from guidelines published by the CBI for its member companies) who perceive that it is in their best interests to start releasing information to employees.

The need is to produce a 'company information policy' dealing with the provision of information to employees. Because it is increasingly recognised that board-level involvement is important for industrial relations, it is further recommended that the information policy be approved by the board and continuously monitored at that level.

Many companies already have an information policy. There is, however, no one satisfactory model, and whatever policy a company adopts must be developed in the light of its own situation and requirements, taking into account such facts as the size of the company, its structure and activities, the characteristics of the work force, and existing negotiation and consultation arrangements.

In general terms, and subject to legal requirements, it must be the responsibility of senior management to decide what information should be made available to employees, and how and when such information should be provided. It is recommended that in developing an information policy steps should be taken to discover what views employees at all levels hold on this matter since it will not always be possible for senior management to be fully aware of all needs. It is particularly important that the views of middle and line management should be taken into account. This may be done by the use of attitude surveys or questionnaires (in larger companies) or by formal and informal meetings with employees. A piecemeal approach to the provision of information, or over-selectivity as to what is to be provided, may be self-defeating. Whilst it may be legitimate to draw distinctions between information which employees are required to have by law and that which they need in order to carry out their jobs efficiently, it might be a mistake to assume that employees are interested only in information of direct and personal relevance to their individual position and work in the company (though this is certainly true of many). Indeed, provision of information on this restricted basis would probably not be in the company's own interest because it would not necessarily encourage employees to identify themselves with the company as a whole.

Administrative constraints may arise where the amount of work and expenditure involved in the compilation and assembly of information is out of all reasonable proportion to the value such information would have. Certainly there are other powerful and legitimate constraints on the provision of information: constraints such as confidentiality, fear of competitive disadvantage and breach of Stock Exchange regulations. The work force needs to be made aware of these constraints and to be sympathetic to them. They should not, however, be regarded as justifying a generally restrictive approach. Companies should bear in mind whether the consequence of failing to provide information might not be more damaging in industrial relations terms than the danger of such information becoming common knowledge.

A company information policy should contain a list of the types of information to be provided to employees. The following checklist, which is adapted from a CBI policy document, is designed to highlight the kind of information particularly useful in an inflationary climate. Clearly there are others as important in a general and continuing situation. Items marked with an asterisk are those where constraints of competitiveness or confidentiality may arise.

Information about the Company as a Whole

Organisation of the Company

Company activities

Organisation of the company in relation to its subsidiaries or holding company (if any)

Unit structure

Management structure up to and including directors

Product range

General company objectives and policies

Finance

Turnover

Profits (including the effect of inflation on conventional figures)

Dividends

Losses

Liabilities

Total fixed assets

Details of directors' remuneration and emoluments

Details of chairman's remuneration and emoluments

Total wages and salary bill

*Total labour costs as a percentage of operating costs

*Administration costs as a percentage of total costs

*Costs of materials

Competitive Situation and Productivity

Export performance
Details of main national and international competitors
Competitive possibilities
Orders, production and marketing situation
*Production schedules
*Work levels and standard performance levels
*Labour costs per unit of output
*Savings arising from increased productivity

Plans and Prospects

*Mergers and takeovers
*Investment and expansion
*Closures
*Changes in location
*Research and development
*Product changes

Information Relevant to Employment

Manpower

Average numbers employed
Numbers employed by sex, grade, occupation, department, etc.
Labour turnover, redundancies and dismissals
Absenteeism
Redeployment, training and retraining
Days lost through disputes

Industrial Relations

Grievance procedures
Safety rules, policies and programmes
Health and welfare matters
Disciplinary and dismissal procedures
Trade unions
Recruitment and promotion policies and methods
Working rules

Pay and Conditions

Rates of pay
Notice periods
Hours of work
Holidays
Sick pay
Pension schemes
Results of negotiations affecting pay and conditions
Principles and structures of payment systems
Job evaluation systems
Profit sharing, stock option and saving schemes
Life assurance schemes
Average earnings

INFORMATION RELEVANT TO THE IMMEDIATE WORK SITUATION

Comparative departmental production figures
Comparative achievement of targets
Changes in the working environment

If this advice is heeded by companies it may well be that the widespread adoption of company information policies will turn out to be a useful by-product of the present inflationary age.

NOTES AND REFERENCES

1. Price Commission, *Report for the Period September 1–November 30 1974*, HMSO (London, 1974).
2. 'At a time when world prices are rising, the threshold itself boosts inflation. As I shall show later it sets limits to the extent to which a Chancellor can use indirect taxation as a means of raising revenue. It is as if I have been sent into the arena to fight the monstrous problems now confronting me with one hand tied behind my back.' Denis Healey, Budget Statement, 26 March 1974.
3. For example, Aubrey Jones, *The New Inflation: The Politics of Prices and Incomes*, Penguin Books (London, 1973); Alan Fels, *The British Prices and Incomes Board*, Cambridge University Press (Cambridge, 1972); and H. Clegg, *How to run an Incomes Policy* (*and why we made such a mess of the last one*), Heinemann (London, 1971).
4. 'The retail price index has risen 25 per cent over the last twelve months to May 1975 and 32·3 per cent since February 1974. The change over the last three months, grossed up to an annual rate is 53·1 per cent . . .' Mrs Shirley Williams (Secretary of State for Prices and Consumer Protection), House of Commons, 16 June 1975.

5. See *Money International*, 28 March 1975.
6. *Counter Inflation Act 1973*, HMSO (London, 1973).
7. *Price and Pay Code, Consultative Document*, Cmnd 5247, HMSO (London, 1973).
8. *The Attack on Inflation*, Cmnd 6151, HMSO (London, 1975).
9. H. Behrend, 'Attitudes to Price Increases and Pay Claims', NEDO Monograph 4 (London, 1974).

CHAPTER 4

Controlling Procurement Costs in Inflationary Conditions

DAVID FARMER

The most significant element in manufacturing costs is materials. To be more precise, manufacturing companies, on average, dispose of more than half the money they receive from sales in purchasing materials, components and services. As one measure of comparison, labour costs represent something over 20 per cent, less than half the proportion attributable to materials. Thus, despite the considerable irritant of fast-rising wages, at the level of the manufacturing company, materials loomed largest as the most significant contributor to inflation during the period 1973–4.

In considering the problem of controlling procurement effectively in inflationary conditions, it is as well to start by attempting to learn something from the 1973–4 experience. After all, British management has had limited experience of handling high rates of inflation with respect to material costs. In the event few managers were prepared for the turmoil which developed during 1973–4.

As far as procurement was concerned, if we are to judge by a major survey undertaken by the present author,[1] few companies had considered supply as a strategic element in their planning. The events of 1973 and 1974 resulted in a hasty review of that attitude by many companies. Yet, sadly, at the time of writing, with fairly generally accepted predictions of continuing worldwide economic downturn, some companies are already reverting to former attitudes. In some cases this reversion has been prompted by the change in the supply–demand balance which the downturn has brought. But the basic importance of effectively managing procurement remains unchanged. Indeed, if the expectation of some informed opinion on inflation levels for the quinquennium to come are realised, the significance of materials as a proportion of manufacturing costs may become even more important. The author has argued elsewhere[2] that there is an urgent need for managements to take greater note of materials in their planning. Inflation at current levels emphasises that importance.

CAUSES OF INFLATION IN MATERIAL COSTS

What were the principal causes of inflation in material costs in the UK during 1973–4?

Firstly, there were large rises in commodity prices. These were caused by high levels of economic activity coupled with real or 'engineered' short falls in supply. These increases were reflected in raw material and component prices of all kinds. Secondly, the effective devaluation of sterling against other currencies exacerbated the problem as well as affecting the majority of imported materials and goods other than commodities. Thirdly, despite price legislation, there was a tendency for suppliers to attempt to increase profit margins, or at least to maintain profit ratios, which had the effect of inflating profits *pro rata* with other cost increases. These attempts to increase profit margins were, of course, a natural reaction of suppliers trying to take advantage of their dominant position in times of shortage. Fourthly, there were substantial increases in labour, financing and other costs, which suppliers wished to recover wherever possible from their customers. Fifthly, buyers, faced with an indiscriminate pattern of rapid increases in prices in conditions which emphasised supply lead-time, became increasingly less price sensitive.

Aspects relating to these causes will be examined in this chapter in discussing possible approaches to the problem in hand. And throughout this discussion the main thesis will be that much can be done, and could have been done, by improving efficiency in the procurement area.

PROCUREMENT

Despite its unfortunate connotations, the term 'procurement'[3] is now accepted as implying much more than the traditional 'purchasing'. Procurement involves the management of the flow of materials and parts from suppliers through the manufacturing plant. It involves quality, time and inventory management as well as price. It implies close liaison within the organisation in order to attempt to minimise total costs while meeting other corporate objectives. It includes close collaboration between colleagues from procurement and other areas, from the design stage through to final production. Overall it suggests the need for a level of management in the procurement area which contributes markedly to the achievement of a better cost–effectiveness balance throughout the organisation. In consequence the discussion which follows seeks to consider the problem in hand as an integral part of a system and not as some isolated function charged with obtaining goods as cheaply as possible.

Some readers may feel that the breadth of such involvement is outside the scope of any one function. However, the present task is to consider ways in which we may effectively control procurement costs. Thus the intention is not to inflate the importance of any *function* but rather, among other things, to illustrate the negative effect of the conflict that exists among sectional objectives regarding materials. That conflict, not infrequently concerned with lack of information, is a prime cause of unnecessary cost in the materials area.

COMMODITY PRICES

It is beyond the scope of the present discussion to attempt to forecast changes in specific commodities, or even to suggest tactical or strategic approaches to particular markets. Neverthless, given their importance in inflation, it is necessary to consider some aspects of activity in the commodity area.

During the period 1973–4 the most significant impact on inflation resulted from the action of the Organisation of Petroleum Exporting Countries (OPEC). Since then there has been considerable discussion about the potential of other commodity cartels to inflate their prices in the same manner.

It will be recalled that a group of producers acting in concert engineered an acute shortage in the supply of oil, in conjunction with which they inflated the price of their product by a factor of four. Whatever the long-term price position on oil, and there is much discussion about this at the time of writing, the effect of the OPEC action on the cost of a wide variety of materials was considerable. Furthermore, it occurred over a very short time span. Despite the previously apparent massive power of the oil companies, the producing countries were able to increase their prices significantly.

It has been argued that other producers could harness their own power in a similar way. However, apart from phosphates, attempts at forming producers' cartels have so far been largely unsuccessful. Nevertheless the probability of such action needs to be carefully considered on an ongoing basis, and not only by commodity buyers. Secondary buyers need to evaluate the risks and uncertainty surrounding the commodities which affect them. There is a need for them to develop their product strategies with such aspects clearly in mind.

Informed opinion[4] at the present time suggests that a piecemeal investigation of a number of commodities indicates that very few are in a position comparable to oil. However, a note of caution is sounded by most writers concerning the propensity of producers to coerce and the need to monitor the situation continually. Nonetheless 'engineered' shortages tend to be short-term phenomena. The state of readiness of consumers and their ability to utilise alternatives may be the key to 'weathering the storm'. For the individual company the correct strategy will be to attempt to minimise reliance on the supply of commodities where the probability of such action is high. In some cases this may be impossible; in others, however, an emphasis on selective strategic stockholding or on the development of viable alternative sources of supply or substitutes, or both, can be extremely successful.

Examples of action of this kind which has been taken in the past include replacing copper in electrical fittings and the development of synthetic rubber. The real significance of the former effort was realised following the price advances in copper of 1966. Clearly, developing new technology is often a long and expensive process, but the *recognition* of over-reliance on a particular commodity will enable the options to be evaluated. 'What if . . . ?' questions in the development of strategies are as vital in the procurement area as anywhere else.

It is also true that in the past shortages of a particular commodity have resulted in producers expanding production. Not infrequently such developments have 'come on stream' at a time when consumption has been low, with the effect of forcing prices down. Thus a careful evaluation of prospects in particular fields is essential. Companies which operate in the commodity markets tend to undertake such analyses as a matter of course. Secondary users should utilise this market expertise as a basis for their own decision-making. Much can be gained from their suppliers in the way of intelligence, and commodities are given wide coverage in the press and in journals.

To revert to the question of substitution it is interesting to note the effect of synthetic rubber not only on the price behaviour of the natural substance but also on manufacturing costs and product features. In turn this illustrates the overall effect of material factors on a manufacturing organisation. Synthetic rubber, developed as a matter of wartime necessity, was delivered to users in a loosely baled crumb form. This was much easier to handle and process than the irregular-shaped 'belts' of natural rubber, and there was a resultant improvement in plant utilisation. A further feature of the synthetic product was its controlled quality, which up to that time had not been possible with natural rubber. In turn this allowed tyre manufacturers, for example, to produce a more uniform product with clear market advantages.

Another form of 'substitution' with often considerable economic advantages is recycling. While this is a well-known source of materials, its potential in some areas may be far greater now than it has been in the past. Costings undertaken some time ago need to be carefully re-examined in relation to current conditions. Much has been made of the potential savings in energy which can be made by recycling certain materials as against initial production. From the individual company's viewpoint the cost-saving potential of recycling could warrant initiatives which will act as a useful hedge against inflation. Energy consumption used in the conversion may not directly affect the companies concerned, but given present energy costs the potential effect of such savings on the recycled product cost itself may be significant.

STOCKHOLDING

The possibility of strategic stockholding has been mentioned in conjunction with commodities. The business situation which prevails at the time of writing has made many companies aware of the impact of stocks on their liquidity. However, there are enough cases on record of financial problems related to stockholding to warrant a brief comment here.

One effect of the inflationary situation during 1974 was that the value of stocks greatly increased. However, working capital had to be increased to replenish stocks and high interest rates made stockholding more expensive. For example, whereas a rule-of-thumb cost per annum of 25 per cent for holding stock was accepted when interest rates were in single figures, it would not be unreasonable to argue that the interest rates which applied at the end of 1974 necessitated a revision of this yardstick to 35 per cent or more.

Thus a strategic stockholding policy needs to be considered against costs of this nature. It would take a substantial increase in the buying price of the goods involved to offset such costs. Nonetheless strategically it may still be prudent to maintain 'hedge' stocks. But it should be recalled that such stocks have their main purpose in helping the company to 'ride-out' engineered shortages. In cases of genuine shortage and price inflation, such stocks can only provide temporary respite. This is not to say, however, that stockholding cannot be helpful to the company in a financial sense where the latter conditions apply.

Stocks are the most obvious area of attack in cases where costs are being squeezed. They are the favourite zone of activity of consultants charged with quickly improving company liquidity. They have the advantage, too, of being relatively easy to measure against a variety of norms (e.g. stockturn). Much has been written about stock control methods, and readers will be able to draw upon considerable experience as well as the relevant literature in considering management action in this field. Certainly it is an important area of manufacturing management at any time. In inflationary conditions it is even more important to control stocks effectively. Thus, while not dealing with specific techniques in this section, it would be advantageous to mention a number of potential actions which may assist in minimising material costs.

In the first place it is worth stressing the seemingly obvious fact that it is not the average stock levels across the board which are the key to efficiency. Rather it is the specific control of key stocks. The basic 'A, B, C' method of stock management is important in this work. However, it is also essential that stocks are monitored on a continuing basis to obviate obsolescence or to take account of planned programme changes, or both. All this necessitates careful liaison between, for example, procurement, marketing, production and suppliers. Having the right stock at the right time is often a function of information availability. Costs can be minimised if procurement are able to give suppliers adequate notice of change and can work with them and colleagues to 'flatten' demand. In a simple sense stocks may be looked upon as insurance. Thus they can be reduced in volume if the likelihood of supply failure is itself reduced.

Then, given necessary levels of mutual confidence, stock costs may be minimised for both supplier and buyer through, for instance, the use of the 'consignment stock' idea. Here a supplier stores his produce on the buyer's premises and the buyer pays for the goods as he uses them. There are clear advantages to the buyer, but the seller can also reduce his own costs by this procedure. Firstly, he has a guaranteed market for the goods he delivers. Secondly, the process of invoicing/stock checking which is involved improves his liaison with the buyer. Thirdly, he is utilising customer's premises to stock his own product with considerable potential savings, given the expense of warehouse area. Fourthly, he can minimise handling and transportation costs.

One example of this approach concerns a timber importer and a customer who uses fairly large quantities of certain grades of timber. The costs which the importer carries in cases where he is not able to sell the timber ex-ship include handling and transportation charges to his yard, storage charges in his yard and, subsequently, the handling and transportation charges incurred in taking the timber to the user.

In the case in question the importer arranged to deliver the material direct from the ship to the user's yard. The user was required to store it but was only required to pay for the timber when he used it. Both buyer and seller gained from the arrangement in that costs had been eliminated which otherwise would have had to be included in the selling price. From the particular seller's viewpoint not only were some handling and transportation costs avoided but also, with his own storage capacity already taken up, he would have needed to hire additional space to accommodate the timber.

LIAISON WITH SUPPLIERS

The consignment stock idea suggests that there may be more mutual cost-saving opportunities which liaison between buyers and sellers could promote. It is the opinion of the writer that closer collaboration between some buyers and sellers could prove to be a potent management tool in fighting inflation. It is wrong to assume that a reduction in a selling price need necessarily mean that the seller must accept a reduced margin. Specifications, transport and handling methods, and delivery volumes and frequencies are but a few examples of areas where mutual analysis can be beneficial. Without reducing the opportunity to source elsewhere, buyers should be seeking ways of collaborating more effectively with their suppliers.

One aspect of buyer–supplier liaison which has been a feature of the more sophisticated relationship in procurement is the so-called 'open book' system of price negotiations. This system has allowed significant purchasers access to their suppliers' cost data and manufacturing arrangements, a basic objective of the system being that buyer and seller work together to eliminate unnecessary cost. Where the buyer has more back-up services available to him, this liaison could include advice on, for example, improving manufacturing methods or reducing scrap rates.

When this scheme was first introduced in the UK some sellers saw it as another 'weapon' to reduce their profitability. However, properly managed it can produce, and has produced, significant cost savings. For example, the author was involved with one case where the supplier was not able to keep to schedule because he was scrapping three items in every ten. Apart from the volume/delivery problems which arose as a result, in order to produce a reasonable level of profit the price of the product had to be inflated to recover the cost of scrapping. Discussion between buyer and seller eliminated several problem areas in the specification and improved the manufacturing method. As a result, scrappings were reduced in a short time to an acceptable level. The effect on cost was remarkable. The seller actually increased his profit level, yet the selling price was reduced by almost 20 per cent. Significantly the liaison was forced on both parties. The buyer had had similar troubles with other suppliers and the company in question was threatening to abandon the project because it was unprofitable. Clearly not all liaisons will produce such startling results, but the principle of this kind of collaboration can be beneficial in most cases.

A significant contribution can often arise from a careful examination of specifications, particularly when they have been developed by the buyer. Application of value-analysis techniques can be of considerable help in this respect. Cost comparisons based upon current information can also be helpful (including the often hidden aspects of delivery difficulties with certain materials or components). Yet another potential area of action is to consider current manufacturing technology related to the design of the product. In other cases it will pay to ask the simple question of the supplier, 'Do you have a standard item which performs the same function?' 'Specials' are always more expensive than standard items and it is surprising how often a buyer specification is produced unnecessarily. In these cases the buyer does not know of the standard and the seller is not aware of the specific function that the item is to perform.

This type of approach may be thought of as 'defensive' cost reduction; there are possibilities, too, in action in a more 'positive' direction.

For example, despite the excessive levels of 1974 inflation, manufacturers in the hand-held calculator field have been able to reduce their selling prices markedly. Lower component prices stemming from improved technology in the supply market were a significant factor in allowing this action.

INTERNAL LIAISON

Once again, this suggests clues to the involvement of materials and procurement management in the total operation of a manufacturing concern.

Given the escalating cost of development during inflation and yet the need to develop new products, an important function of management is to ensure that the new product gets to the market as quickly as possible. Development times of three to seven years are not uncommon, and those concerned with materials, tools, patterns and other purchases may be seen to be an area of potential reduction in these periods.

Much of the pertinent action in this area can be related to effective procurement planning and management in the pre-production stage. Indeed, examination of supply difficulties will often show inadequacies in pre-production management. In many organisations a major reason for such difficulties is that procurement staff do not become involved early enough in the planning stage. Among resulting problems which increase costs are inadequate lead-time for sourcing, monopoly sources and, in turn, inflated buying prices which pre-empt future as well as present negotiations. These problems may be exacerbated where there are several stages in the development of the item concerned, for example, tooling, pattern equipment and samples, where a delay in any one may have a detrimental effect on the subsequent stages.

In one organisation where this type of problem was common, a consultant found that the procurement department were spending the bulk of their time on 'remedial action'. Because of schedule difficulties buyers were trying to source quickly, trying to reduce supplier lead-time and inevitably finding themselves in a poor bargaining position. Apart from anything else the philosophy became 'get it at any price, we'll beat them down later'. There were additional problems, too, in that quality control suffered at various stages as systems were short-circuited to ensure delivery. Inevitably with the emphasis on 'fire-fighting' there was little time to think and plan.

On close examination of the company structure the consultant found that there was no liaison between the product development department and procurement. If it was necessary to obtain information from the supply market, this was done by the people in product development. Even that was limited, however, and the group tended to make assumptions about availability and price based upon their experience. Naturally their main focus was upon the engineering problems involved.

The consultant had been called in originally because the company's sales department was concerned that it was losing sales because of their inability to get the product to the market place at the planned time. In addition, there were problems with products during the introductory phase mostly, so it was believed, to do with manufacturing quality. Inevitably, the investigation through engineering, production and quality control suggested a variety of reasons for difficulties which were appearing at various stages of manufacture. Not surprisingly, some of these stemmed from supply problems at the various points in manufacture.

Among other things the consultant's report recommended that procurement should be represented at product development discussions at the conceptual stage of the product. A procedure was developed which was regarded by all parties as an unqualified success. It is an idea well worth considering as a tool not only to help combat inflation but also to smooth and reduce development time and get the product into the market earlier.

The basic idea as far as lead-time is concerned is that, using pertinent information and working backwards from the planned launch date, procurement indicate when they require drawings, releases, etc., to meet the programme. The design/development programme is then structured around these key dates.

Another economic advantage of the system has been that procurement staff have provided information at the conceptual stage. This has enabled designers to take a value engineering approach, with considerable success. A further benefit has emerged in that better team planning has enabled procurement to instigate a series of supply market reviews. They have developed dossiers on components and materials in a number of fields and have combined these with other data to help forecast developments in the markets concerned.

This case illustrates the potential of better materials management in manufacturing. It is indicative of the level of involvement which will not only eliminate unnecessary costs but also help a company to become more competitive in its own market place. This increased competitiveness will arise partly from being able to launch products more effectively, particularly as regards lead-times. In turn this may be important to customers in, for instance, their own programme planning and could result in reduction in inventory and work-in-progress. Where inflation is affecting business to current levels the economic importance of this kind of relationship to both buyer and seller cannot be overemphasised.

COST/PRICE ANALYSIS

In previous sections the idea of buyer–seller liaison to help eliminate unnecessary costs has been put forward as having considerable potential in managing materials in inflationary conditions. It may be thought of as contradictory in the sense that traditional commercial attitudes have suggested overt conflict between the two parties, the buyer attempting to minimise buying prices while the seller strives to maximise his profits. Yet, as has been said earlier, current practice, particularly in monopoly–monopsony relationships, includes the use of open book price negotiations. This involves the buyer and seller agreeing the make-up of the selling price, including material, labour and overhead costs as well as profit levels. Clearly this is not always possible, but the potential of such liaison in eliminating costs can be considerable.

In respect of manufactured purchases at least, much can be done by the buying organisation without the direct collaboration of sellers. In effect the buyer attempts to calculate the price that the seller should charge. He produces an estimate which may be used as a 'target price'. The availability of this information places the buyer in a stronger position in his negotiation, in that he has a yardstick against which to measure the price offered by the seller. This kind of information can be invaluable in inflationary conditions where the market price sensitivity of buyers is eroded by frequent changes.

To illustrate: one company has built up a library of information on its supply markets and, more specifically, its major suppliers. Records include all price increase requests from this group, together with the levels awarded for the last eight years, labour and material cost trends for the same period, and supplies price data built up from negotiations over the period in question. Considerable information is available regarding specific industries, and the specialist procurement staff seek to monitor the effect of inflation on their own operation, particularly with regard to time lags (and hence stocking policy, etc.). These forecasts are distributed to product managers so that they may be aware of potential changes and the date when they are likely to take effect. The report shows annual and effective rates, cost increase requests by material groups, and those which (i) have been accepted, (ii) are being investigated, (iii) are being negotiated and (iv) are expected.

THE EFFECT ON SUPPLIERS

Despite the current levels of inflation the company concerned claims that sellers have tended to make 'more reasonable' increase requests in recent years than at the time the scheme started. The buyers claim that they are able to substantiate this view in part by the fact that the difference between actual payment and that requested was greater in previous years than in 1974. In 1967–8, for example, the actual payment was 45 per cent of that initially requested; in 1973–4 it was 71 per cent.

While these data could be interpreted as indicating that the buying company was *less* effective during this last year, other evidence would suggest otherwise. (This includes rates paid by the company compared with similar firms; their own estimates of price movements; and cost trends monitored over five years against published data.)

It is interesting to note that the levels of inflation over the last five years are seen as the prime motivation for the level of activity of this analysis department. Its work is seen by the whole management team as sharpening their awareness of the impact of materials on the company operation. If it can be argued that prices are a function of information, then significant buyers should build similar data banks. Even if external benefits are ignored, increased awareness throughout the organisation of the potential effects of better materials management can itself contribute markedly to cost reduction.

GOVERNMENT ACTIVITY AND PRICES

It is not the intention to discuss Government controls in the pricing area in this chapter; the topic is dealt with elsewhere in this text.[5] However, it is worth stressing that the Government service has developed considerable data on prices and trends which are available to buyers. Whatever their limitations or those of the legislation which surrounds them, they provide invaluable guidelines, as do other published data from Government sources (e.g. the Department of Industry Price Index). The quarterly reports from the Price Commission are also invaluable as an aid to more effective materials management.

The basic point to bear in mind is that the Price Commission is extremely well equipped with data since it has a statutory right to detailed cost figures. However, the volume of price movements is so great that it is not possible for the Price Commission to deal adequately with even the majority of them. Thus buyers should use the services available together with their own data to explore continually ways in which suppliers' costs and prices may be reduced.

FIXED PRICES

One of the many procurement problems which inflation has brought with it is the reluctance of suppliers to enter into fixed-price contracts. This policy is understandable in that suppliers, faced with considerable cost uncertainty, have been unwilling to fix their prices for any length of time. An interesting fact is that fixed-price contracts have been used for many years and through previous periods of inflation (albeit more gentle). Consequently it is the writer's opinion that procurement staff should work towards restoring fixed-price contracts whenever possible. Even though it may only be feasible to arrange such contracts for relatively short periods, it could help to stabilise the position. Once again it is necessary to take a specific rather than a generalised approach, for it will be easy to establish such arrangements in some cases and extremely difficult in others. The problem for the seller, of course, is uncertainty over his costs, which again suggests the importance of liaison between the two parties. On the other hand, a danger from the buyer's viewpoint could be that the seller, if forced to agree to a fixed price for a period, will attempt to cover himself against all eventualities. This could result in an artificially inflated price. Nevertheless firm orders, longer lead-times and ongoing collaboration on specifications, among other things, can help to minimise uncertainty and costs to mutual advantage. Another important factor will be mutual trust and a free flow of pertinent information between the parties. However, all this should be undertaken within a thoroughly commercial framework, where both parties are seeking a realistic price agreement.

CORPORATE PLANNING

A conclusion of the survey mentioned earlier[6] was that the majority of manufacturing companies in the survey group did not include consideration of procurement matters, at least at the strategic level, in their longer-range plans. And yet supply problems can threaten the survival of such companies.

The events of 1973 and 1974 forced managements to pay greater attention to this area, but that action was largely 'fire-fighting'. Nonetheless these events did result in an awareness of the inadequacies of supply data in many organisations. In some cases that inadequacy was reflected in the quality or quantity or both of staff working in the area. In many companies a related problem was that there was no mechanism to generate the right kind of data. More commonly, the attitudes of the staff concerned and their top management emphasised short-term goals. Procurement was seen most often as operating at the tactical rather than the strategic level, the budget rather than the plan.

The basic point to note from all this is that while no system, plan or technique could have obviated all the many complex supply difficulties of the period in question, most companies should have been better prepared. That lack of preparation must, surely, have contributed to inflation. Just as it is essential in the marketing area to plan with a view to taking advantage of opportunities while obviating difficulties, so it is in procurement. There is just as much uncertainty in the environment, and the elements in the environment are similar.

Effective longer-range planning in the procurement area will involve such areas as:[7]

The external environment	(including technical development and market structures)
Supply strategy	(including competition for resources, source vulnerability, inventory levels, etc.)

Product development and product life (liaison with R & D; inventory suppliers)
Source development (including new sources, capacities of existing sources)
Make or buy (relating to own facilities planning market changes, labour supply, etc.)

In more stable conditions each of these areas may be extremely important to the survival of the company. In inflationary conditions they can take on greater importance as the company strives to ensure profitable survival in an uncompromising world.

MAKE OR BUY

When a company wishes to obtain supplies of a particular component or material there are basically two sources of supply open to it. It can either obtain its requirements from another company or make them itself. While a great deal has been written about the subject, in practice such decisions are frequently made in a less than objective manner and often against questionable data. While there are limitations regarding what it is possible for any company to make, this is an area of investigation which can prove to be extremely beneficial, particularly in inflationary conditions.

Manufacturing involves decisions to commit capital for potentially lengthy periods, not only with regard to a particular process but also in peripheral activities. Because of greater sophistication in many industries, and inflation, it will also involve increasing capital commitment as time goes on. In addition, it suggests utilisation of management and other resources, possibly on an increasing scale. Since the basis of any strategy must be to utilise company strengths against competitive weaknesses, such dissipation of resources (financial, facility and management) needs to be very carefully considered.

Clearly in planning terms the decision must be to utilise available resources in the most effective way towards the achievement of company objectives. When an outside source is chosen the company will seek to concentrate on those things which it is best placed to do, whilst using outside resources where they prove to be economically and strategically attractive. The crux of the matter is where to concentrate company effort, and the variables relating to the decision are wide ranging and complex.

Among the more crucial variables are the increasing sophistication and polarisation of supply markets, the companies which make up those markets and the activities of competitors in them. The financial, technical and political characteristics of these markets now and in the future necessitate careful evaluation of the company's own situation together with the likely activities of competitors. It is clearly necessary to be able to develop an ongoing appraisal of changes in the future external environment.

Other aspects of the evaluation as it relates to the development of this area of strategy include consideration of development of minor sources to obviate monopolistic (and potentially inflationary) strategies of major suppliers, and market research intelligence about the viability of existing sources. Where there is cause for concern with particular suppliers, one option might be to integrate vertically either formally or informally, which may be thought of as a 'make' or 'buy' decision.

The foregoing discussion is included here to illustrate some of the facets to make or buy decision-making. For present purposes it is worth stressing again the fact that many prior decisions to buy or to make need careful appraisal *now* in the light of *current* conditions. It is probably true to say that most companies are currently buying some things which they ought to be making, and making some things which they should be buying. However, when examining particular situations with a view to making the company more cost effective, it is extremely important to have in mind the strategic implications of the decision. A particular decision may be attractive in the short term, whereas in the longer term it could place the company in a disadvantageous position. Nevertheless, despite the difficulties involved, the potential of the make or buy area is worthy of serious attention as one factor in the management of materials in inflationary conditions.

CREDIT

One of the more overt effects of the 1973–4 inflation as far as industrial buyers have been concerned relates to the pressures which suppliers have brought to bear on credit. Whereas previously it was not unknown for larger organisations in particular to take four months' credit or more on purchases, suppliers, faced with liquidity problems, are now working to reduce these periods. Clearly with interest rates above 15 per cent per annum, even a one-month reduction in the time it takes to pay is worth $1\frac{1}{4}$ per cent. It has been argued that even though suppliers have given long-term credit in better times they have recovered the cost of that credit in their selling prices. If this is true, and it would appear to be a sound argument, prices would need to be inflated simply to allow for the extra cost of financing the capital involved.

Apart from any other factor, this is an area where buyers can work with suppliers to their mutual advantage. Relatively prompt payment is an attractive factor to the supplier, and it could well be a means of the buyer obtaining a reduction in selling prices in return for this facility. In particular where suppliers have liquidity problems they will be prepared to consider inducements in return for relatively prompt payment.

Clearly the buying company will need to weigh the advantages of early payment against the disadvantages of the negative effect on their own cash flow. However, usually there will be occasions where the idea will prove advantageous to both parties, although this will be where the buyer is in a strong cash-flow position. In addition, from the buyer's viewpoint such an arrangement could be used to advantage in negotiating a fixed-price contract.

Another aspect of credit relates to the viability of suppliers. Paradoxically, it could be beneficial in the long term to help to ensure that certain suppliers remain viable in the short term. Most bankruptcies are shown to be related to liquidity problems, and smaller suppliers in particular are vulnerable in this respect. If they are faced with such difficulties at times when order books are diminished they could succumb.

While it is a matter of judgement as to whether or not to offer support in such cases it can be important to bear in mind the structure of the supply market. If the company goes out of business, what alternatives are there? Are those alternatives competitive? Have they monopolistic tendencies? Will there be sufficient capacity to meet needs when the market improves? Questions of this kind can be helpful in arriving at a decision. If a decision is made to offer support in some way, then apart from the strategic implications it would suggest the possibility of both parties working together to minimise and stabilise prices.

One example of such support involved the buying company contributing to an investment in plant at the supplier's works. It was able to guarantee a base load for the plant, the price of which was calculated against an agreed formula. This 'joint venture' approach proved to be so successful that the buying company is currently looking for other ways of using the idea. Both managements claim that the venture has been an effective exercise in minimising mutual costs. While the idea may have a limited application it is indicative of the kind of mutual problem-solving approach in which many more buyers and sellers might indulge with advantage. Such collaboration may be very important as regards new plant, where joint ventures may well be a means of eliminating some of the uncertainty. Given current levels of inflation, it might also be one way to ensure that capacity is available when the market picks up.

OTHER COURSES OF ACTION

1975 was widely predicted to be one of the most difficult years from the trading point of view since the war. While levels of inflation in the UK were thought to be beginning to fall in the face of industrial recession, redundancies, closures and short-term working were affecting a wide range of industries. In such an environment, what other actions should buying companies take to minimise the effect of inflation?

At a recent seminar conducted by the writer thirty senior procurement executives took part in a 'mini-delphi' survey. The method used to conduct the survey was extremely simple, in the sense that there was only one 'round'. Several of the ideas which emerged have already been discussed, but the following views are also worth consideration.

- Reduce stock levels generally but increase selected ranges.
- Reduce buying horizons on downturn.
- During downturn, use resources to develop alternative materials/suppliers in order to take advantage of competition when the upswing occurs, especially where currently single-sourced.
- Develop wider knowledge of market upon which to base strategies (suppliers/competitors—potential and actual).
- Examine material specifications and alternatives, being careful to use today's data in any comparison.
- Examine possibility of 'mutual co-operatives' to minimise cost rises (e.g. between three or more parties (buyers) or on a reciprocal trading basis (buyers and sellers)).
- Put greater resources into recycling area, but with careful evaluation of forward scrap supply situation. If going ahead, aim to guarantee supplies with long-term contracts if there is any doubt about quantities available.
- Consider booking capacity as a means of (i) ensuring supplies, (ii) helping the supplier to minimise uncertainty (e.g. a base load in a process plant), (iii) allowing attractive buying prices on a longer term (possibly fixed) basis.
- Sound strategic buying, capacity booking or contracting during the downturn in business should result in attractive buying terms.
- Take the opportunity during downturn to develop data banks and associated buying information systems. Since information is a key factor in decision-making there is a need for the right data at the right time to decide on appropriate action. Speed of reaction to market trends will be a key factor in attempting to contain inflation in the procurement area.
- Keep up to date on Government counter-inflation legislation and work with suppliers to contribute to that effort. Understand the services available as well as the rules.
- Carefully consider comparative currency values (today and into the future) when sourcing abroad. Revaluation or devaluation or both can have a considerable inflationary effect.
- Improve controls and cost monitoring information.

- Examine intra-plant handling and transport with a view to minimising costs.
- Examine potential of nationalisation/standardisation programmes.
- See what can be learned from South American experience.

CONCLUSION

In concluding this chapter it is necessary to stress what is probably the most important factor in combating materials price inflation: that is, that it is vital that procurement people should not regard inflation as inevitable, for this increases their propensity to accept price increases. Procurement staffs should see their role as key to countering inflationary prices—not unilaterally, but in collaboration with colleagues and suppliers alike. Companies should seek 'aggressive creativity', with all staff concerned with materials looking for ways to reduce costs while meeting functional requirements on a continuing basis. Top management should recognise that inflation necessitates greater rather than lesser resources being applied to procurement, for during such periods much more is required of the function. For example, information systems and forecasting have to be improved upon if the supply market is to be monitored effectively. Then, given the shorter-term fluctuations, better calibre people will need to be available to interpret and decide on specific action—faster. Despite the need to accept shorter decision horizons in some respects, procurement should contribute to longer-term plans with the right quality and range of data.

Finally, while inflation is a key problem for management at this time, it should be recognised that it is but one of the elements in the supply market 'equation'. There are several basic factors which interact one upon the other and which should all be borne in mind in any analysis. Clearly the supply and demand factor has an important part to play. The relative power of the parties in the market is another main factor, while a third is currency exchange rates and their effect on purchases from other countries.

The emphasis of this chapter has been on the management of industrial materials and components. Little has been said about capital purchases, with the particular difficulties associated with contract prices and long lead-times. Suffice it to say in the present context that the concept of supplier–buyer collaboration may also be essential to success in capital equipment transactions, with one vital area of attention being the reduction in the authorisation time by buying companies from the date of quotation to placing orders.

In the end, the requirements of management in inflationary conditions are fundamentally no different from those which apply at any other time.

The differences which do exist are primarily in the pace and frequency of change and in the need to react more quickly not only to events but also to signals in the environment before such events occur.

While general in approach, this chapter has endeavoured to develop a practically oriented discussion which will suggest a variety of considerations for management about improving performance in the important area of materials supply. Materials could be the most significant sector upon which management should concentrate in the fight for business survival during the next five years.

NOTES AND REFERENCES

1. D. H. Farmer, 'Some aspects of source decision-making *vis-à-vis* corporate plans in UK-based multi-national companies', unpublished doctoral dissertation, the University of Bath (1973).
2. D. H. Farmer, 'Corporate Planning and Procurement in Multi-national Firms', *The Journal of Purchasing and Materials Management*, Vol. 10, No. 2, May 1974 (USA); and D. H. Farmer, 'The Impact of Supply on Corporate Planning', *Long Range Planning*, March 1972.
3. The terms 'procurement' and 'materials management' are deemed to be interchangeable for present purposes and are used as such in this chapter.
4. See G. F. Ray, 'Raw Materials, Shortages and Producer Power', *Long Range Planning*, August 1975; and Monatsbericht 'Märkte', No. 5, 22 May 1975, Institut für Wirtschaftsforschung/ETH (Zürich).
5. See Chapter 6, 'Pricing Strategies to Cope with Inflation'.
6. Cf. D. H. Farmer, 'Some aspects of source decision-making *vis-à-vis* corporate plans in UK-based multi-national companies'.
7. For a full checklist relating to the procurement area of corporate planning', see D. H. Farmer and B. Taylor (eds.), *Corporate Planning and Procurement*, Heinemann (London, 1975), Chapter 2.
8. See Herman Schneider, 'How Inflation has changed the Purchasing Man's Job', *Procurement*, July 1974, which illustrates the considerable limitation of such a comparison.

CHAPTER 5

Marketing Under Conditions of Inflation

CHRISTOPHER WEST

Inflation affects all aspects of corporate activity but marketing, which operates at the interface between supplier and customer, is likely to experience the sharpest pressures of all. For marketing not only is subject to the same escalation in costs affecting other departments but also has to take into account changes occurring in the market environment in order to fulfil its primary purpose of attracting and holding customers at prices which will yield the company an acceptable profit. The marketing task, which relates both to the strategic positioning of the company to ensure continued survival and growth and to activities such as advertising, sales promotion, distribution and public relations which ensure that month-by-month budgets are achieved, is particularly susceptible to the ravages of inflation. As prices rise to keep pace with costs and as the customers reappraise their requirements in the light of changing relative values and possibly falling real income levels, marketing has to produce a response which maintains sales volumes and minimises the effects on profits.

Inflation strikes at the marketing process from two directions. The most important of these is that inflation distorts the existing relationship between buyers and sellers and thereby creates uncertainty over current and future trading practices. Inflation also affects the cost of the marketing function itself. As a highly labour-intensive activity, marketing is very sensitive to spiralling wage and salary levels, but transport costs and packaging, printing and communications charges also have a major impact on the cost of marketing.

In marketing terms everything commences and ends with the customer; he is, to paraphrase Adam Smith, the sole purpose for corporate activity. This chapter will therefore take as its starting point the effects of inflation on markets and customer behaviour. It will then examine how marketing activity can respond to the changes induced in the best interest of the company, and will conclude with a discussion of how marketing costs can themselves be constrained to the minimum. Pricing, which is evidently a key component of marketing activity in an inflationary environment, is not discussed in detail; the subject is of such vital importance that it is covered separately in the following chapter.

HOW INFLATION AFFECTS MARKETS

Inflation, particularly at the rapid rates experienced since 1973, has a number of primary and supplementary effects on the markets for goods and services. Customers tend to be highly responsive to rising prices, particularly when they cannot be passed on to third parties by demanding either higher wages from employers or higher resale prices for goods or services supplied. Price is one of the basic roots of the relationship between buyers and sellers, and although a major function of marketing activity is to shift the focus of customers' attention from price to the benefits that the seller is offering, the final decision on whether or not to buy and which supplier to buy from is nevertheless heavily conditioned by the customer's perception that he is obtaining value for money. Once standards are set any forces, whether internal or external, which affect the price at which sellers can offer their goods or services must therefore have a fundamental impact on the suppliers' position within the market. The strength of the impact varies according to the magnitude of the changes occurring and variations in the competitive situation. If a firm raises prices unilaterally in a competitive market environment and product quantities and associated services remain the same, a simple realignment of customers towards the lowest cost suppliers can be expected, although it does not inevitably follow. When all suppliers raise prices or if the high cost suppliers convince customers that the premium is worth paying for the additional benefits that are obtained, then a realignment of customer loyalties may be avoided.

If all prices, costs and incomes inflated at the same rates so that the differentials between products, services and sectors of the community remained similar, then the effects of inflation would be minimal. Larger volumes of money would be required to complete transactions, but there is nothing fundamentally unsettling about that. There may be some temporary shifts in purchasing as customers, feeling that their traditional suppliers have become more expensive, try alternative sources; but if the differentials are in fact unchanged a full or partial reversion to former purchasing patterns normally occurs.

The principal problem in an inflationary situation is that the adjustment process to a given increase in costs is invariably uneven. Prices of some products rise faster than others, and while the incomes of some sectors of the community are able to keep pace with rising costs, and in cases overtake them, others lag behind. The uneven progress of costs, prices and incomes distorts market relationships possibly out of all recognition, and although market pressures may at a later date restore the original balance, by then customers' requirements and purchasing practices may have altered permanently.

When copper prices rose to unprecedented levels in 1972–3, major copper users such as the electrical industry sought substitute materials and switched part of their demand to aluminium. Having discovered the new material and worked with it there was no wholesale and immediate return to copper when prices fell again. By drastically raising crude oil prices the Arab Governments provided a favourable environment for the exploitation of oil reserves previously regarded as being of marginal economic interest. Once established, however, production from these sources will doubtless continue, if only for strategic reasons, regardless of trends in the price of oil from OPEC countries.

All organisations, companies, Governments and households endeavour to maintain a balance between their income and their expenditure and, in fact, will normally aim for a surplus of income over expenditure in the form of savings or profits. In an inflationary situation, when there is a tendency for costs to rise faster than incomes, savings and profits may be eliminated until adjustments in income bring the equation back into equilibrium. During the adjustment period the organisation can sustain its operations by drawing on reserves, by borrowing or by trimming expenditure levels. The first two courses can normally be pursued for limited periods only, that is until reserves are depleted or credit limits reached. Expenditure adjustment will follow with customers possibly reverting to previous expenditure patterns after the income adjustment has occurred. All of these forces must be taken into account in a marketing programme.

The major effects of inflation can be identified as follows:

- An increased sensitivity on the part of customers to price.
- A heightened resistance to marketing blandishments.
- A tendency to substitute for quality products those which, although of a lower quality, are regarded as adequate.
- An increased resistance to non-essential features of products.
- A shift in expenditure away from non-essential goods and services.
- An accelerated desire to stockpile products for which a substantial price rise is foreseen.
- A destocking of readily available goods to reduce stockholding costs.
- A reduced rate of growth in real demand for goods and services.
- An increased requirement for value for money.
- A highlighting of certain sectors of the market as offering continued profit opportunities or suffering least from inflationary effects.
- A change in the importance of alternative distribution channels.

Price Sensitivity

Increased sensitivity to price in the purchasing decision is a seemingly obvious effect of inflation but is nonetheless important for that. Marketing activity attempts to concentrate purchasers' attention on product benefits and value for money, and anything which counteracts this effort makes the task of the marketeer more difficult. Price sensitivity manifests itself by more determined efforts to shop around and an increased willingness to trade off product quality against price. Some aspects of marketing activity will fall prey to this trend. For example, the loss leader may become the sole object of a visit to a retail outlet and not the magnet for a broader range of purchases that it is intended to be. In industrial markets the willingness of a customer to consider alternative suppliers may be increased, and where previously there was an element of inertia created by the loyalty to existing suppliers in view of the benefits that this brings, this may be outweighed by the price advantages of moving. Thus the position of an established supplier may be more easily challenged.

Falling demand for a product is not, however, an inevitable sequel to rising prices. In 1974 flour prices were approximately 50 per cent higher than the 1973 levels, yet demand for flour was rising rapidly. The reason for this was that the cost of prepared foodstuffs and eating out had also been rising steeply, although not always by as much as the rise in flour prices, and home cooking was the most effective way for households to trade down their purchases. Consumers react therefore not only to individual increases but also to overall trends in the total basket of goods that they are required to purchase.

Value for Money and Real Benefits

Inflation tends also to change the basis on which customers assess products. Value for money has always been a primary criterion by which alternatives are assessed, but as prices rise customers are likely to test that the benefits offered are both real and required. In other words, they are less likely to take a supplier's word when making claims for his products or services and more likely to test it for themselves. Spurious claims will be more readily identified, and the supplier who takes positive steps to demonstrate that what he has to offer represents good value for money, for example by introducing a value engineering service, will enjoy a marketing plus.

Customers are also likely to take a more liberal view of product values Lower purchase prices may be outweighed by higher installation and running costs. The availability and cost of servicing, the average downtime and the servicing intervals can all become key issues that are fed into the value-for-money calculation.

Non-essential Products and Product Features

Inflation will tend to strike hardest at the marginal product, the last one to be added to the list of requirements as incomes rise. In private households this may be a luxury item without which life may be less pleasurable but can nevertheless proceed—the second car, the fur coat, the hi-fi set. In industry it can strike at the products which improve working conditions without adding to productivity—the drink-vending machine, the power sweeper or the new office carpeting. The difficulty for the marketeer lies in the definition of what is marginal, since few customers will perceive products in the same light; one man's luxury is another man's essential and decisions will be made accordingly. As living and working standards improve values change and what was once regarded as a luxury may have become an essential; similarly, what was once regarded as essential may have become dispensable. Many families would rather reduce their food intake than dispose of their television set, and firms experiencing severe difficulties in holding together their labour force may find that their social facilities are more essential than new productive plant.

The automobile is a significant example of a luxury that over the years has come to be regarded as an essential by large sectors of the population. A recent survey carried out by BP Marketing showed that motorists turned a blind eye to soaring automobile running costs and would rather sacrifice cigarettes, holidays, clothes, entertaining and home improvements than give up the use of their cars.

In terms of the products or services sought on the market place inflation induces a trend towards the utilitarian at the expense of the luxury. In order to stretch their budgets customers are likely to reduce their commitment to individual items to the minimum. Thus raw detergent becomes more attractive than the perfumed variety available at a price premium, pre-prepared convenience foods lose out in favour of basic ingredients for home cooking, the compact car and the standard model will attract some customers away from the de luxe models. These trends run counter to any ambitions to increase the level of up-market trading but enhance the profit-earning potential of those products that can credibly claim to be low-priced substitutes.

The buyer of industrial goods, particularly capital plant, is generally more restricted in his choice of alternatives, but he too will be subject to the same cost pressures. Liquidity problems may force him to accept an inferior product with a shorter life in the hope that by the time replacement is due the business climate will have improved. He will also look more critically at the range of his purchases in order to eliminate those which make no contribution to productivity or profit. He may become less concerned with appearance when to achieve an attractive finish the supplier is demanding a higher price.

Stocks

The traditional attitude to stockholding may change radically both among consumers and among industrialists. In some cases inflation can encourage stockholding, for example, when customers anticipate further massive price increases there is a tendency to purchase ahead of requirements and to stockpile. However, this trend may be tempered by a heightened awareness of the cost of carrying stocks in terms of both the cost of the capital tied up in them and the cost of the storage space. Throughout the present inflation manufacturing companies have run down their stocks on a massive scale, although this reflects not only their awareness of the cost of stockholding but also their lack of confidence in future trading levels. The position may be further confused by a common supplementary effect of inflation—shortages. Each shortage as it occurs is likely to cause a build-up of stocks as customers guard against it happening in the future. It is worth noting that rumoured shortages (and, indeed, rumours of major price increases) can have the same effect as real shortages—as with the phantom British salt shortage of 1974. In that case stocking of salt took place on such an incredible scale that an actual shortage occurred at retail level, thereby reinforcing the trend. Customers' attitudes to stocks and the consequent periods of stock building and stock depletion that can occur tend to result in marked cyclical variations in the demand for the products affected.

Reduced Real Demand

The methods employed to control inflation invariably result in stagnation and, in many cases, a depression in real demand for goods and services. The effect is to increase the level of competition in the market place and to squeeze the marginal suppliers. As has been indicated, changes in demand levels will be uneven; while some sectors are likely to experience drastic cuts, others may remain stable or even increase depending on customer requirements and the postures adopted by supplier companies. Falling demand levels and increased competition place a downward pressure on prices which runs counter to the inflationary trend. The effect is, however, inevitably temporary, since firms cannot survive loss-making situations for long and must either raise prices or cease trading.

Distribution Channels

Distribution channels will feel the effects of inflation through the actions of both suppliers and customers. In seeking the lowest prices consumers will gravitate towards the distributors offering them. Thus the discount trader, regarded in the past with a certain amount of suspicion as a distributor of inferior products, often in less opulent surroundings, is likely to receive the benefit of a strong upturn in influence even if located in less accessible locations than the high street stores. Comfort and convenience are easily sacrified for cost advantage by customers. There is also likely to be greater interest in dealing direct with the manufacturer where possible, thereby cutting out the middle man and his mark-up. The longer waiting time or the necessity to buy in larger volumes becomes less of a handicap if the cost savings that result are significant.

MARKETING ACTION IN AN INFLATIONARY SITUATION

In all business environments the key to survival, growth and profit lies in the creative anticipation of change. Inflation accelerates change and thereby creates a situation which threatens the weak but provides the strong and the adaptable with a multitude of opportunities. The well-run marketing department thrives on change and is in a unique position to adapt the company's operations to an inflationary environment. At the same time inflationary pressures within organisations produce a requirement to cut costs, and marketing costs are all too often a ripe target. Very little of the marketing action proposed in this section is unique to an inflationary situation but lies within the normal compass of marketing activities. However, inflation heightens the need for certain marketing actions, and it can be argued that at a time when there are strong pressures to reduce all forms of corporate expenditure, marketing activities should be strengthened to combat threats and capitalise on opportunities.

Marketing's contribution to corporate survival during times of inflation can be summarised as follows:

- The use of research and other marketing resources to monitor changes.
- Initiation of innovatory product developments and product modifications to profit from changes caused by inflation.
- The introduction of segmentation strategies to concentrate corporate activities on those areas of the market which continue to offer profit opportunities.
- Deployment of promotional effort to offset the adverse effects of rapidly rising prices on sales.
- Adapting distribution strategies to market changes induced by inflation.
- Setting pricing policies which accord with cost, market and competitive conditions.

Monitoring Change

The creative anticipation of change requires firstly that the changes that are occurring in the market place are known, their effects monitored, and market trends predicted. The marketing department has at its disposal the necessary antennae for achieving this either through the sales force or through the deployment of market research resources. Both should be in a position to feed back precise information on what is occurring among customers and competitive suppliers and to provide a basic input into the market planning process. The function should not be purely passive. In order to take advantage of change the reporting process should seek out profit opportunities as well as provide information on which an inflation-proof marketing strategy can be based. The specific information that can be fed into market plans by those in closest contact with customers includes:

- Competitors' pricing policies, promotional strategies and product modifications (such as range rationalisations, new models).
- Trends in total spending on the products supplied.
- Effects on inflation on product preferences of customers and product substitutions.
- Effects of inflation on customers' ability to pay.
- Customers' reactions to price rises.
- Changes induced in distribution channels.
- Importance of price in the overall decision-making process.
- The firm's image in the market place relative to that of competitive suppliers.

Such information is vital to judge the response required from the firm in the light of both customer requirements and the activities of competitive suppliers. In order to gather it the firm must organise the activities of the field sales force to ensure that there is a procedure for collecting information on a regular basis, for the analysis of the data for market planning use and for circulation of the results to the appropriate personnel. The use of salesmen to collect data is an apparently cost effective solution to the problem though they can introduce an element of bias into the results and would not be good salesmen if they did not. A more effective substitute is market research personnel, either employed by the company or used on a consultancy basis. The market knowledge gathered must have a strategic purpose. It is wasteful of both time and money to collect data that may be interesting but cannot be applied to any valuable purpose. The three areas in which marketing can make the most valuable contribution towards profiting from inflation, and therefore the principal subjects which should be covered in any information collection exercise, are product policy, the definition of new segmentation strategies and the deployment of the various promotional and distribution resources available to the company.

Product Policies

As shown in the previous section inflation will strike at the product requirements of customers in various ways, namely in volume terms, values and in sourcing requirements. In other words, customers may buy less as their real incomes fall, buy less expensive versions or buy from alternative (cheaper) sources. To protect against any adverse impacts of these trends on the company's activities, and even to enhance the company's ability to attract customers away from competitors, the marketing department can initiate product developments which capitalise on the fundamental changes occurring within the market. These may vary from the introduction of utility versions of products which dispense with the frills and offer better value for money to a complete revamp of product features. In recent years the automobile industry on both sides of the Atlantic has been reversing its traditional model policy by concentrating on smaller, more efficient and more functional vehicles. In doing so they have recognised that lower purchase prices and running costs have begun to outweigh luxury in the evaluation criteria of customers. The recent boom in the demand for semi-finished foodstuffs, bake-yourself bread, home-brewed beers, marmalade and jam mixes, represents, at least in part, another creative response to the rising prices of finished products which leaves the consumer with the satisfaction of feeling that he has contributed to the production process and thereby saved money (even if in fact he has not).

Segmentation

The unequal effect of inflation on the different sectors of the economy and groups of population creates the need for a finer segmentation strategy. Segmentation focuses firms' attention on the product and customer groups which offer the greatest profit or growth potential. It is an important element of marketing strategies at all times, since few organisations can afford to attack every market opportunity with equal vigour, and should therefore concentrate their efforts on the prospects that are likely to prove most worthwhile. Inflation is likely to accentuate the differences between the opportunities offered by the various sections of the market served, and thus companies should adopt a policy of seeking out those of their clients who are least affected by inflation and concentrate their marketing efforts upon them. As a general guideline the customer groups that are likely to be least affected by inflation, and therefore in a better position to maintain their expenditure levels, are:

- Those that are in a position to protect their own incomes from the effects of inflation, for example Government departments for whom tax income rises in line with earnings or firms whose incomes are indexed to inflation.
- Those who by virtue of their activities feel the effects of inflation later than others, for example when wage costs are the main inflationary driving force capital-intensive industries feel the effects later than labour-intensive industries.
- Those who are quick to recover from or adjust to inflationary pressures.

The task of the marketing department should be to identify the customer groups least affected by inflation at any point of time and to focus corporate attention on them until such time as they are displaced by other groups. As the effects of inflation roll through the economy, a flexible segmentation strategy is required, although to avoid long-term damage to the company's marketing programme care must be taken not to antagonise customers by letting them know that they have been down-graded to a lower priority group.

International segmentation can be as important as a segmentation strategy within the home market. Not all export markets have been equally affected by inflationary pressures, and indeed the oil-producing countries have benefited from a massive inflow of resources brought about by the rise in oil prices. Thus at times when other countries are experiencing recessions the oil producers have been expanding their rates of consumption and drawing in ever-increasing imports of products. The marketing implications are simple, although often difficult to implement: companies with suitable products to offer should devote a higher proportion of their marketing resources to those countries that still have money to spend. The problems of mounting an export programme, particularly by those with no previous experience, can be severe, but the rewards in both the long and the short term can more than compensate for the effort.

In addition to its positive role, marketing also has a negative function in an inflationary environment when selecting the customer base for marketing activities. The corollary to identifying the most profitable customers is the location of those which should be avoided. Inflation can have an unfortunate effect on cash flow, and even if certain customers do not actually face bankruptcy their payment intervals for goods or services received may lengthen considerably. A customer is not a customer unless he can pay for the goods, and for all suppliers rapid payment is more attractive than slow payment if excessive credit costs and cash flow problems are to be avoided. By monitoring the trends within the industries served and by making limited enquiries about specific customers, the marketing department can make a valuable contribution towards avoiding payment embarrassments with customers. The results will not be infallible, but any reduction in bad debts is valuable.

Promotional Effort

In addition to being a source of information on markets, the marketing department is also the major channel through which information flows out to present and potential customers. The means by which companies communicate with their customers—advertising, public relations, exhibitions—can have a major effect on the view customers have of the company and its products, and the creative use of these channels is vital in an inflationary situation. Much of what customers believe about products and services stems from what the suppliers themselves say about them in addition to direct and indirect experience.

Inflation tends to disorient customers and, by invalidating the traditional standards by which they evaluate their purchases, can lead to a rapid build-up of false impressions, particularly over prices. A common feature of an inflationary situation is for customers to believe that prices are rising faster and more frequently than is in fact the case. The promotional tools of the marketing department can be used to correct such impressions, and indeed an overt attempt to demonstrate that the company cares about customers' views on prices will invariably have a beneficial effect on customer attitudes. However, the theme should not be taken too far, bearing in mind that a major function of marketing activity is to persuade customers to buy the company's products by means other than price blandishments. The promotional campaign should seek to keep the full range of product and service benefits in the forefront of customers' minds and, by implication, the question of price in the background.

Distribution

In the light of changes caused by inflation the marketing department should carefully examine the company's distribution strategy and seek to match it more closely to customers' purchasing patterns. This could involve some breaks with tradition, such as the acceptance of discount traders as customers or the introduction of direct sales to selected customers, but if not considered there is a risk that the company will be left stranded by an obsolete distribution strategy.

It is equally true that certain distribution techniques may be rendered ineffective by rapidly rising costs. Highly labour-intensive door-to-door deliveries have, for example, been kept alive by competitive pressures and the fear of a customer reaction if discontinued. However, as costs rise the ability of suppliers to maintain them and the willingness of customers to pay for them are likely to become increasingly doubtful. By spotting the moment at which a change in distribution methods can be effected the marketing department can make a major contribution to eventual cost savings.

Pricing Strategy

The development of a pricing strategy is probably the most fundamental of the roles that the marketing department has to play in an inflationary situation. This role is discussed in detail in the following chapter, but it should be stressed here that it does not cease once prices, margins and discounts have been set. It then becomes necessary to ensure that the policies are adhered to. In any marketing and distribution relationship other than direct contact between supplier and customer it is possible for intermediaries to distort manufacturers' pricing policies to the extent that the original objectives are negated. Carefully prepared pricing policies can all too easily be upset by arbitrary decisions made by retailers and wholesalers. This can be minimised by policing distributors' activities via such means as a prices audit as well as by making manufacturers' pricing policies clear to the final customers, who can then judge for themselves the effect that distributors are having. The practice of advertising recommended prices is becoming increasingly common in consumer goods markets, often with the implied statement that by shopping around it may be possible to purchase at a lower price. In this situation the recommended prices become maximum prices and the risk of sales being lost through retailers charging a premium is minimised.

MINIMISING MARKETING COSTS

Everything said so far in this chapter implies that marketing expenditure should be increased during times of inflation and therefore that marketing departments should be excluded from any cost-pruning exercises that are undertaken. Nothing is further from the truth; marketing is as prone to wasteful expenditure as any other department—some would say more so—and a careful review of marketing costs is essential when companies are searching for avenues to increase levels of profitability. The principal problem that will be encountered in any such activity is that, unlike other functions, in the case of marketing the benefits for a given level of expenditure can very rarely be computed. Often the only method of demonstrating the effect on sales revenue of any given marketing expenditure is empirical, i.e. to start or stop doing it; then, if the effects are negative, it is too late to correct the situation. Nevertheless with marketing expenditure accounting on average for some 12–15 per cent of sales revenue it is a sizeable target for any cost-cutting programme.

Six concepts for the minimisation of marketing costs can be identified. They are:

- Minimisation of the objectives and targets for the company's marketing programme.
- Careful selection of the market segments that are to be attacked.
- Subcontracting of non-recurring functions.
- Minimisation of the marketing payroll.
- Selection of the most cost effective marketing techniques.
- Sharing costs wherever possible.

The first two points have been covered in the previous section of this chapter, and suffice it to say here that by applying a budgetary discipline to marketing activity it may be possible to force marketing departments to concentrate on those sectors of the market that are likely to yield the highest returns, provided that the resources allowed are consistent with the sales targets that are set and the company is not too obviously attempting to squeeze blood out of a stone.

A simple device for both cutting overheads and increasing the effectiveness of marketing activity is to subcontract all functions that are required on a sporadic basis. Research, advertising, direct mail and public relations services can all be adequately supplied on an *ad hoc* basis by specialists, and provided that the annual expenditure on them does not exceed the total cost of employing in-house staff there may be both a saving and a more efficient marketing operation. Outside specialists may not know the internal business of the company as well as their in-house counterparts but by virtue of their specialisation are generally efficient, and the cost can be dispensed with as soon as there is no further requirement for their services. It goes without saying that this approach enables a company to minimise its marketing payroll. Many marketing departments can be run quite efficiently by a manager and a field sales force drawing on outside consultants for specialist inputs. They tend to grow by taking on in-house specialists who, once employed, quite naturally tend to fill their time to the full, and even take on assistants. The staff may well be justified by the magnitude of the task that is being undertaken, but as higher costs begin to bite it is time to appraise critically the resources that are being deployed. It may be that a reallocation is required rather than any cuts in marketing staff and, if so, it is also appropriate to ask whether the personnel themselves are right for the jobs they are fulfilling. As companies and staff grow older there is a tendency for positions to be filled by increasingly senior staff. Could these more expensive personnel be more efficiently employed elsewhere in the organisation?[1]

The marketing techniques employed should also be critically reviewed in times of rapidly inflating costs. The inflationary process inevitably distorts the relationship between costs, and what may once have been a highly cost-effective technique may have lost some of its advantages. Marketing techniques can be placed on a scale of costs, which increase according to the inputs required per customer, or potential customer, contact made. Thus personal selling with a heavy time involvement for each contact may be regarded as being considerably more costly than advertising, which with a single printed message can reach an audience of millions. Of course, the impact made by the different approaches also varies, the mass communication techniques tending to be less persuasive than those tailored to individual recipients, but as costs rise the trade-off between cost and impact can work in favour of the lower cost marketing techniques. For example, a business traditionally employing a sales force to service customers and collect weekly orders may find it profitable to separate the servicing and order collection components of the task and to employ a smaller force of sales representatives to carry out the former and telephone sales girls to do the latter. Telephone contact with customers is considerably quicker than personal visits and the overall cost of the sales function may be reduced drastically.[2] If telephone charges themselves rise steeply, consideration may then be given to some form of postal ordering system.

Attention may also be given to improving the effectiveness of the broad-ranging (buckshot) marketing techniques such as direct mail and exhibitions. These have lost favour in recent years as marketing departments have sought to adopt a more direct marketing programme aimed at specific targets. However, by devoting more time to exhibitions and direct mail, and sometimes more money, it is possible to up-grade them to a level somewhere between personal selling and their original position and turn them into more cost effective techniques. For example, in recent years there has been considerable interest in mobile exhibitions which can be used to reach specific target groups in different regions of the country. The utilisation of the exhibition material is considerably higher than that constructed for the one-off national or international exhibition, and in some cases the choice of vehicle and approach has been such as to ensure a high degree of interest from the target groups. In 1974 and 1975 Philips used a well-known sailing boat as a floating showroom for a range of computers which attracted a wide audience at the ports it visited. The experiment was judged a great success by the company.

A further technique for minimising marketing costs is to share expenditures wherever possible with other organisations. Many marketing functions can be carried out on a shared cost basis, and jointly sponsored research projects, joint advertising campaigns and jointly operated sales forces have become increasingly popular as costs rise. There is always the risk that a shared marketing programme may work more to the advantage of one partner than the other, but it is also possible for the joint programme to be more effective than any singly mounted effort could be. The partners in a shared cost programme may be comparative organisations such as distributors working with manufacturers or manufacturers of different products purchased by the same customer groups. They may also be competitive organisations sharing the same markets.

When attempting to cut the cost of the marketing programme it is important to bear three criteria in mind. First, will the cost saving achieved reflect in the overall profitability of the company? There is little point in cutting costs if the overall effect is to reduce the company's earnings below what they would otherwise have been. The extent to which this would happen is dependent on the second criterion, namely will the cuts so dilute the marketing effort that the company's ability to dispose of the goods or services produced is seriously weakened? Cost cutting is worthwhile only in so far as it improves the productivity of the marketing activity; when productivity can no longer be improved, further cuts will result in lower sales.

The third criterion is that cost cutting should not seriously threaten the company's future business. Short-term survival is, of course, important and the future can to a very large extent look after itself. However, some cuts may so alter the marketing organisation that the long-term business of the company is threatened. New product development can be a lengthy process and any gaps in the development programme may be difficult to recover, resulting in a retarded growth pattern in future years. Similarly, any fall in standards in distribution and the service levels offered to customers can cause the build-up of an image of inefficiency which may take years to eradicate.

CONCLUSION

The marketing process thrives on change, which itself generates both opportunities and threats. Marketing skills should be deployed to capitalise on the opportunities and avert the threats. Inflation at rates recently experienced in the Western world has brought about more changes in markets than has occurred in the previous decade, and adapting to the new order has placed a major strain on the marketing resources of all companies. At the same time there has been pressure to reduce marketing and other costs incurred by companies. The rationalisation of these two conflicting requirements is likely to produce a fundamental change in the nature of marketing activity itself. Many activities developed during times of normal inflation will be exposed as wasteful and there will be more encouragement to develop highly cost effective marketing techniques. For the marketing leopard to change its spots could prove a painful process, but the exercise will provide the function with a much needed opportunity to prove its worth in ensuring long-term corporate survival.

NOTES AND REFERENCES

1. See R. N. Skinner, 'Organising for Marketing on a Small Budget' in Christopher West (ed.), *Marketing on a Small Budget*, Associated Business Programmes (London, 1975).
2. See J. L. Wage, *How to Use the Telephone in Selling*, Gower Press (London, 1974).

CHAPTER 6

Pricing Strategies to Cope with Inflation

RICHARD SKINNER

For many companies inflation may offer at least one major benefit. It brings into sharp focus what has hitherto been a comparatively neglected area in overall business strategy, that is the prices and terms on which a company's products are offered, and in doing so it provides a stimulus to rethinking basic policies which are related directly to net profit and survival in any set of economic conditions, inflationary or otherwise.

It is perhaps unlikely that pricing will be recognised as a neglected aspect of business without further explanation. Long before inflation reached its present proportions the importance of price was accepted by most executives concerned with marketing, and the relevance of price to profit margins was taken as self-evident. Nevertheless a distinction may be drawn between the perceived importance of an activity, measured perhaps by its prominence in any discussion of company results or by the numbers involved in it and their status within the company, and the amount of real thinking and decision-making it attracts. It is quite easy to become conditioned to believing that there are certain areas of admitted importance where there is little scope for change however much thought is given to them.

Recent research[1] indicates that this has until lately been true of pricing, which, in the industrial field at any rate, has been a matter of rule-of-thumb routines and *ad hoc* decisions—albeit top level *ad hoc* decisions—rather than an essential part of the business plan. It is routines of this type which are breaking down under the pressure of inflation, leaving the way open for a radical reappraisal.

This chapter will therefore take as its starting point the state of the pricing art in a pre-inflationary context, making use of the research findings now available, and then go on to examine the changes made necessary by inflation, the opportunities the present situation may provide and the ways in which future pricing policy may be influenced by the experiences of both sellers and buyers over the next year or two.

In order to be as clear as possible in dealing with a rapidly changing state of affairs it may be as well to make a few definitions in advance. By the *pre-inflationary situation* is meant not a period when there was no inflation, but a time in which inflation proceeded at a more moderate pace and a real growth in profits was still generally achievable. There is more than a difference of degree between an inflation rate of 5 per cent and one of over 20 per cent. The effect of the latter on business requires a completely fresh approach to problems which may always have existed to a lesser extent. This is reflected in what is described as the *present situation*, inflation at the steeper rate with which the United Kingdom has become familiar during 1974 and 1975. It covers what may come to be seen as a comparatively early phase of a new development in the relationship between buyer and seller.

When the *next stage* is discussed a further change will have been postulated, and the situation envisaged is one in which the initial adjustment to inflation has been made by both sellers and buyers and it becomes necessary to consider how pricing activity will have to be conducted in a context of continuing inflation, shrinking demand and increasing competition.

PRICING IN A PRE-INFLATIONARY SITUATION

Much has been written on pricing, or perhaps it would be more accurate to say on pricing models, as a result of the central position of the subject in economic theory. Economists have not, however, succeeded in bridging the gap between the theory of the price mechanism and what might be called the mechanics of pricing practice. Simple models of competitive or monopolistic situations and their variants cannot be expected, and are perhaps not intended, to describe what actually happens in such a large and complex area of human activity.

Accountants in writing on the subject have adopted a more pragmatic approach and have contributed a good deal of useful discussion on costing methods. Costing, however, falls short of pricing, and again a gap appears which has not in most cases been bridged satisfactorily.

More recently mathematicians have entered the lists, with attempts to bring probability theory to bear on the bidding situation. Some quite complex models have been constructed, but these techniques are not in regular use, although they may hold some promise for the future. Psychologists have also been active and have conducted limited research into consumer buying behaviour related to price. As a result of these developments the accepted theory of, for example, demand curves has been modified in several interesting ways.

Marketing men and general managers responsible for pricing policy have by contrast been somewhat reticent in print, although often giving the impression in conversation that accepted theory may have little relevance to the day-to-day problems with which they are faced. Research[2] has shown this reaction to be based on more than mere prejudice. Pricing practice, in the industrial field at least, is paradoxically both more complex and less sophisticated than pricing theory would indicate.

In the first place companies may have many hundreds of products to price, and may sell them through more than one channel of distribution. Some prices are published, others are calculated by means of purely internal lists or formulas, and still others are produced to meet tenders or to suit the requirements of individual negotiations. All may be subject to discounts which could be varied by category of customer or quantity ordered, either at one time or over a period.

People in a wide variety of different job functions may be concerned in establishing prices and they tend to approach the job on a rule-of-thumb basis. Most prices are based on cost, and the cost is subjected to an uplift in one way or another. Nevertheless prices established in this way may subsequently be modified, and margins on individual products vary. When a modification is made to a cost-based price the reference point appears to be the general level of competitive prices.

It is here that the difficulty of relating economic theory to pricing practice becomes obvious, for there may be grounds for doubting whether companies really know how their competitors are pricing similar goods and services and how high prices could be set without producing an adverse customer reaction. One problem is that competitive products may not be directly comparable. Another is that very little formal investigation is made into competitive prices and customers' acceptance of price. The main source of information, in the industrial field at any rate, appears to be the sales force. This is probably true of consumer manufacturing also, since consumer research appears to have concentrated on the reactions of the end user rather than on those of the manufacturer's immediate customer. Traditional pricing theory implies not only comparatively undifferentiated products but also a perfect knowledge of market pricing. In fact, products are often as widely differentiated as the sellers can make them and market knowledge is clearly far from perfect.

One of the more striking research findings is that the vast majority of industrial manufacturers believe that their prices are either about average for their industry or above average. Only 7 per cent believe their prices are below average (Table 6 .1,). The implications of this apparently

Table 6.1 Comparison with Competitors' Prices, for Different Types of Product Sold

		Type of product sold		
	Total	*Capital Goods*	*Components*	*Materials*
Higher than average	41	50	39	28
About average	48	38	48	63
Lower than average	7	8	8	6
Not stated	4	4	5	3

Figures shown are percentages (base 220)

illogical conclusion are far reaching and will be discussed in detail when considering pricing action in an inflationary situation.

In the light of this information it is not surprising to find that few manufacturers use price as a specific marketing plus. Price itself is not something to be advertised or promoted strongly; rather it is a handicap to be carried in the competitive stakes, while the race itself is won by selling the product's benefits strongly, by sales support in, for example, applicational engineering, by the company's reputation and by personal service. In general the price range offered by the sellers as a whole to potential buyers is seen to be limited. It is clearly a bold step to break away from this type of structure either by cutting prices or by increasing them. The result of this is that different industries may enjoy either reasonable or tight profit margins, dependent on historical factors over which the present generation of marketing managers has had no control.

This does not mean that there is no awareness of alternative strategies. Every competent marketing man will be familiar with the concepts of 'skimming' pricing to take the cream from the top of a market, or 'penetration' pricing to secure a substantial share at the expense of higher-priced competitors. The possibility of adopting one or other of these approaches must feature in countless discussions of marketing strategy. What we now know, however, is that in the event radical departures from the norm for an industry are made much less often than might have been supposed. When it comes to settling the actual strategy to be implemented, the argument seems to follow these lines:

- The proposal is to increase price and make more profit. *But* if it is believed that our price is already high in comparison with others, how can we justify this and how can we succeed in raising prices without a disproportionate fall in sales? Customers are used to the present level and it would take a product with really outstanding benefits to justify a higher price.
- The proposal is to lower prices and obtain a greater market share. *But* if we do so, our competitors, whose manufacturing costs are similar to ours, will retaliate in kind. The only result will be a price war with everyone getting the same share as at present but at less profit. Any advantage we might gain would therefore be short lived.

Granted the widespread ignorance of pricing relativity now known to exist, this argument is sufficiently compelling to keep most marketing men more concerned with neutralising the price weapons of competitors than with forging weapons of their own.

Price changes do, of course, take place but usually in response to cost increases, which may be felt likely to affect all competitors equally and which in any case have to be passed on if margins are to be preserved. Even then there may be sales pressure not to be the first to make an upward move. And while cost increases are few and limited in extent a reluctance to react too strongly or too soon is unlikely to cause much harm, provided that the industry as a whole is operating at a healthy level as far as profit margins are concerned. It is, however, clear that in the pre-inflationary situation a number of industries were operating on margins too low to withstand the shock of cost increases on an unprecedented scale, and some prominent companies could not react fast enough to avoid going into liquidation. It is not always possible to say whether mistakes were made in pricing policy or in costing methods or both, or perhaps because of a failure to appreciate in good time the effect of errors in costing and pricing on the financial health of the operation as a whole. What is clear is that in inflationary conditions any mistake in the general area of pricing can prove fatal. It is therefore necessary to identify the policy changes required to meet the new situation and to ensure that action is taken in good time.

CHANGES NECESSARY TO MEET INFLATION

There are four main elements in the pricing process which require attention:

- Costing methods and stock valuation.
- Price fixing and frequency of price reviews.
- Terms of sale and price variation clauses.
- Government legislation.

Some or all of these must have been the subject of a good deal of discussion in boardrooms over the last two years, and in many cases appropriate action may already have been taken. The following comments are intended to serve as a checklist and perhaps to raise the question of whether enough has been done in each specific area to keep pace with inflation.

Costing

The traditional methods are either absorption (or full) costing or direct (or marginal) costing. Both have advantages, the former in relating unit costs and thus prices to the company's total business plan for a given period, the latter in enabling each pricing decision to be based on the costs it will itself generate and so allowing competitive prices to be fixed which will optimise the contribution to profit and 'fixed' overheads obtainable from the market. Both methods are widely used, although in the industrial field at any rate absorption costing tends to predominate. This is because it is much simpler to operate in practice when hundreds or perhaps thousands of different items have to be priced. Standard costs plus a routine uplift or gross profit margin may be considered the norm in industry, although there are many variations on this theme.

In inflationary conditions costs fixed on historical data can rapidly become out of date, and these include those costs which are conventionally described as 'fixed' overheads. Even direct costs are not always so easy to estimate where there is any significant delay between the order and the invoice. Labour rates have been affected by demands for increased wages on a scale and with a frequency that was not anticipated. 'Threshold' agreements have produced changes that exceeded expectation. Material costs and interest rates have risen steeply. In such circumstances neither absorption nor direct costing can be regarded as reliable unless care is taken to anticipate all increases in costs or overheads likely to occur before the goods or services are delivered and payment is made.

One of the most important aspects of 'anticipation' costing concerns materials used in manufacture or goods bought in for resale and held in stock until sold. These have usually been costed at the historic price of acquisition, and this has in the past produced a reasonable result in value terms. If, however, the business is looked at as a continuing process and not a series of discrete sales, it becomes clear that assets will diminish and cash-flow problems occur if this practice is continued for long in an inflationary situation. Every item removed from stock to be used or sold has to be replaced with a similar item. The money for this must come from the sale itself, and if goods are priced on an historic cost basis there may not be enough cash to maintain purchases into stock unless the time gap between buying-in and selling is very short. This may indeed be the case with fast-moving perishable items, but the gap will be much greater where manufacturing cycles are a matter of months, where long-term contracts are involved with delivery some considerable time ahead, or where purchases are made on a batch basis with perhaps six months or a year between batches. In such circumstances it has not been unusual to be faced with purchase costs increasing at 1·5 per cent or 2·0 per cent a month, sufficient to absorb any calculated profit simply in replacing the material sold.

The answer would seem to be to ensure that costs are calculated on the basis of material prices applying at the time of sale rather than at the time of purchase. This might be accomplished by demanding and obtaining from suppliers firm price quotations valid for an established period ahead —not an easy feat in inflationary times—or by estimating what the cost of materials will be at the time of invoicing. If a large number of items are involved this may have to be done by fixing an average rate of anticipated increase and building it in to all quotations. The same action might be considered where labour costs are concerned. Most companies expect an annual increase and might hope to hold rates steady for a year at a time, but in fact the effect of new grading schemes, 'London Weighting', increased expense allowances and similar extras has tended to produce a continuous rise in costs that needs to be considered when fixing prices.

It does not matter that historical costs rather than these inflated figures may be used in compiling the company's accounts. Cost is considered here simply as a factor in establishing the right price, regardless of how it may be handled subsequently.

Price Fixing

The chief requirement in fixing prices in an inflationary situation is speed. Every avoidable delay in making a necessary increase means a permanent loss of profit which can no longer be taken lightly. The factors involved in determining when a price change should be made are anticipated cost increases and competitive pricing policy. Table 6.2 which is taken from the survey already quoted,[3] indicates that these are already the factors most likely to trigger a change. Cost increases are, however, the main determinant, and it seems that more attention might profitably be given to competitive price levels. Any upward move on the part of a significant competitor provides an opportunity for an increase, and although in pre-inflationary times there might have been some temptation to maintain prices in the hope of securing a greater market share, in inflation the risks attendant upon inadequate prices outweigh the possible advantages of sales taken at the expense of competitors. Internal discipline is necessary to establish a policy of matching competitors' price increases and to pave the way for the next step, which involves positive price leadership.

Price leadership is normally only possible for companies enjoying a substantial share of the market, but such companies need not wait for a general upward movement to be started by others. Once it is seen that costs are going to increase and that margins are threatened there is every reason for making a change and for letting competitors know this is happening and the thinking behind it. In the inflationary situation they know that they will soon have to follow suit, and the knowledge that someone else has already made a move may encourage them to act earlier than might otherwise have been the case. Even in markets where competition is fierce and it is doubted whether price leadership would work, the exercise of calculating the pros and cons of an increase will ensure that a decision is at least considered early in the game, not after everyone else has made a move.

It goes without saying that pricing in this way is not congenial to the average sales manager. His part in the pricing process is therefore likely either to be curtailed or to come under closer supervision from the marketing director or, more likely, the chief executive. There are some long-term dangers in this situation should the condition of the market place change radically, but at least during the early months of accelerating inflation the imposition of a policy of rapid price reviews and of price leadership whenever possible will pay dividends, and sales management will have to accept some diminution of its role in policy-making with regard to price.

In compensation for this, early experience shows that small changes made

Table 6.2 Likelihood of Price Changes in Response to Given Situations

	Market prices generally are rising	*Market prices generally are falling*	*Costs are increased*	*Costs are cut*	*Greater profit is required*	*Larger market share is sought*
Very likely	47	15	80	15	39	12
Quite likely	32	38	16	35	39	43
Not very likely	15	40	1	43	15	37
Not stated	6	7	3	7	7	8

Figures shown are percentages (base 220)

more frequently may be more acceptable to customers than occasional heavy increases which may cause buying policy to be reappraised. This partly depends on how often purchases are made, but as a rough guide customers seem to accept 5 per cent or even 10 per cent steps without demur, while larger increases, especially any that appear to exceed the quoted 'cost of living' figure, cause raised eyebrows.

It may be worthwhile establishing a 'pricing calendar' to ensure that reviews are made regularly. Even if no change is appropriate, at least the matter will have been ventilated. Dates and intervals may vary from one product to another and can be made to suit seasonal trends or the input of fresh cost information.

Terms of Sale

For many companies pricing activity does not end with the price to be entered in the quotation document. If delivery is prolonged for any reason, whether the responsibility lies with the selling company or with the customer, the price quoted may be out of date at the time of invoicing. Either the cost of materials or labour rates or both may have risen to levels beyond those anticipated in the original quotation. This creates both a contractual and a marketing problem.

Contractually the answer lies either in limiting the validity period of the quotation, which may be sufficient protection in the case of goods normally held in stock, or in the introduction of a price-adjustment clause. There is, of course, nothing new in either remedy. It is likely that most standard conditions of sale include some clause limiting validity and that at least a substantial proportion may have in addition a statement to the effect that 'prices quoted may be varied in accordance with changes in the cost of raw materials or labour prevailing at the time of delivery'. What is now required is a review of such clauses to make them workable in practice, and a determination to use them regularly rather than to hold them in reserve as a means of recovering profit on orders which may have run into serious difficulties. It is therefore necessary to abandon the practice, which many companies would have felt only right and proper in the past, of maintaining firm prices until the goods are delivered, unless delivery is prolonged unreasonably by the customer. To accomplish this not only must suitable contractual clauses be chosen but attitudes within the company may also need to be changed, and the marketing consequences of applying terms of sale regularly and rigorously will have to be taken into account.

As far as validity clauses are concerned the question which must be asked first is whether they can reasonably be shortened from, for example, sixty days to thirty days. Whether a shorter period is possible depends largely on the type of market involved, and the time required to compile and to evaluate each quotation. Nevertheless the fact that some customers take many weeks to come to a conclusion is not a good test of the viability of a shorter period. The essential consideration is the time that might reasonably be taken in the majority of cases.

Price-adjustment clauses require more thought, since to make them workable on a regular basis implies the application of a set formula. Clauses incorporating an adjustment formula have been in use for many years, and if a suitable wording is found which enjoys recognition and a fairly wide acceptance throughout the industry, this is normally to be preferred to a 'home-made' version open to argument. As an example, the British Electrical and Allied Manufacturers Association (BEAMA) has established a standard CPA clause and offers an advisory service in its application. Some of these recognised formulas may themselves be in need of revision to meet inflation, but the prime consideration must be whether or not the clause can be applied in practice. The selection of a suitable formula and the definition of the circumstances in which it will be written into quotations are not difficult operations, although setting up the administrative machinery to implement clauses of this type on a routine basis requires some planning and may in itself involve additional cost. For this reason it may be felt desirable to set a lower limit to the size of order to which the adjustment procedure will be applied. The same wording can be used on all quotations since the limit may be varied from time to time and, in any case, no customer will quibble if he is not charged extra.

A greater problem is the natural reluctance on the part of salesmen to stiffen the terms of trade with customers from whom further orders might be anticipated. Experience would seem to indicate that salesmen can be brought to accept the necessity of an adjustment clause in long-term contracts somewhat more easily than they can be persuaded actually to apply validation clauses on quotations. They are after all dealing not with customers in general but with individuals who may not, for good reasons always be able to give an instant yes or no. It is therefore natural for them to let the validity date slip past unnoticed or, if reminded of it, to enter a plea that the decision is only a matter of days away and the order is so finely in the balance that any move to review prices now will certainly lead to its being placed elsewhere.

Experience seems to indicate that however plausible such reasons may be they are better resisted. In many cases the salesman concerned may be able to use the possibility of an increase in price to obtain a decision that might otherwise have taken longer. In others the customer may be willing to pay more—in the face of the evidence we now have, how can anyone be sure that his price is really the highest acceptable to his customer? The application of discipline on the validity of quotations is a necessity of inflation, but it may also help to bring forward business and to eliminate the waste of selling effort devoted to the pursuit of lost causes.

Government Legislation

Inflation brings Governments under political pressure to hold prices down, either by subsidies or by controls, or by a combination of both methods. It is important to appreciate the strength of these political factors, whatever opinion might be held of their economic logic. Economically it would not be difficult to argue that a nation's interests might be better served by letting prices find their own level or by stimulating the competitive market forces that act as a brake on increases. Nevertheless Governments will from time to time be swayed by demands for positive action and, in bowing to pressure from the electorate or from the representatives of organised labour, will set up the bureaucratic machinery necessary to produce evidence of action, if not of results. Businesses then have to adapt to the new situation with which they are faced.

In the United Kingdom price controls have been established and operated under the Counter-Inflation Act of 1973 and a number of Orders made subsequently. This legislation places on companies the burden of pre-notifying, reporting or recording price increases and of justifying them in accordance with a formula of considerable complexity set out in the Data Sheets of the Price Commission. The Price Commission is likely to apply its rules more to whole sections of an enterprise or groups of products than to individual products in the catalogue, and the rules involve consideration of the direct costs, overheads and profit of the business as a whole. Every company that is by its size obliged to have dealings with the Price Commission will have to appoint someone to handle the work of preparing its case in the prescribed form. This may be a very different process from that used in establishing actual prices for individual products, and it is probably better to let these two activities continue independently of each other rather than to confuse bureaucratic requirements with commercial decision-making. The type of work involved in dealing with Price Commission business indicates the need to allocate this responsibility to a senior, qualified accountant, with support from the company's lawyers where necessary. No attempt will be made to explain in detail how such a man should go about his job—if he is worth his salt he will have had years of experience in the selection and presentation of figures to the best advantage. He will, however, have to spend a good deal of time on this work, which is in itself an additional cost and a strain on the company's management resources. When his work is done, he will have determined the maximum percentage increase allowable under the rules, and this may be checked against individual prices calculated independently.

It may be that there are instances where the restrictions imposed by the Price Commission have actually inhibited price rises that would otherwise have been passed on to the customer. Certainly companies which have suffered a diminution in profit will be likely to claim that this is, in part at least, a result of Government action. Where large companies offer a limited variety of standard products in accordance with a fixed price list there may be some truth in this argument, but there are whole areas of business where the restraining force of legislation has produced no visible effect.

This is partly because prices are not so easily defined or compared as legislators would like to believe. A great deal of business is done without the help of published lists. Table 6.3 shows that industrial companies use internal price lists or negotiate individually with specific customers nearly as often as they use published price lists. In fact, they clearly use a mixture of pricing systems in many instances. Furthermore, whether prices are published or not they are often subject to discount, and discount structures themselves are as likely as not to be of an informal, and consequently variable, nature. Finally, the product itself may exist in a variety of forms and with a number of options which may or may not be offered. It is therefore doubtful whether in the industrial field there is any check on price which could be applied with consistency or which could not be countered if it were necessary to do so.

Table 6.3 Pricing System Employed

Published (customer) price list	55
Internal price list used for quotation but not released to customer	47
Formal tender	43
Individual negotiation with specific customer	53

Figures shown are percentages (base 220)

Apart from this inherent defect, there is reason to believe that in many sectors of industry the Price Commission has in its first year or so of operation unwittingly encouraged rather than restrained price increases. As has been indicated, the greatest restraint has in the past been the fear of competition. The thought that competitors might not be so quick to react to inflation might have postponed some of the measures necessary to bring forward price reviews and stiffen terms of trade that have already been discussed. Concern over the possible loss of business might have acted to reduce the level of increase proposed. With the establishment of the Price Commission competition came rapidly to mean rivalry between accountants seeking sanction for the largest increases possible. So Government intervention appears to have reinforced the measures listed earlier as commercially prudent. Both the customer and the salesman have in this period exercised less than their usual influence on price, while the accountant concerned with maximising margins has made the running.

In these circumstances it is not surprising that the tangible results of price control are hard to assess. Undoubtedly price legislation has distorted the economic pattern in some areas, and inhibited the commitment of capital and management resources in those industries most affected, but the extent of this dislocation is not easy to measure, nor can we know how prices would have risen had no legislation existed. Whatever temporary measures are taken in future, there are few ways remaining of tightening control in the long term short of destroying the whole concept of a competitive economy, and although a bureaucratic institution tends to create its own momentum it is probable that the Price Commission will play a decreasing part in business affairs as time goes on. It is, in fact, all too likely that more stringent economic circumstances will ultimately put a more effective brake on price increases than any Government body could.

THE OPPORTUNITIES CREATED BY INFLATION

Although the inflationary situation is developing rapidly, and the possible direction this development may take has yet to be discussed, it may be as well at this stage to summarise the opportunities that inflation offers to those companies which are not only prepared to take the steps necessary to meet the problems it brings but are also willing to rethink pricing strategy as a whole.

These opportunities occur both in pricing individual products and in setting pricing policies for the markets in which a company participates. They stem from the disorientation towards pricing which has taken place among customers and salesmen alike. Because they may be short lived they require rapid action if they are to be fully exploited. This is quite consistent with the main message of inflation, which is that decisions and actions must be more rapid than was thought possible or even perhaps desirable in more stable times.

Disorientation appears in the form of vagueness about the 'right price' for an article. In pre-inflationary times this concept was fairly well established and competitors' prices fell within close limits. Buyers could obtain information about the 'right price' from historical data on previous orders, from discussions with other buyers and from competitive salesmen. As soon as changes become too frequent for these sources of information to be reliable, disorientation sets in, accompanied by a diminution of price sensitivity. Whereas previously a 10 per cent or even a 5 per cent deviation from the norm might have resulted in an order being placed elsewhere, the customer no longer has a fixed point of reference. On the contrary, he has an incentive to order now, without prolonged investigation, since next week the price may be higher still.

This phenomenon gives to those companies which are bold enough the opportunity of correcting anomalies in their pricing structure. There are in most catalogues products which are not so profitable as others and which may be carried to support the sale of the main profit-bearing lines. These can now be examined to see whether they cannot be put on the same level of gross profit as other products. The fact that one product is subjected to a heavier increase than others is less likely to cause problems when every price is moving upwards more steeply than ever before.

The knowledge that competitors are having to meet the same inflationary pressures and that their thinking is probably on similar lines may enable the process of anomaly-correction to be extended to markets which as a whole have proved less profitable than required. Either prices can be adjusted or the company has in an inflationary situation to consider withdrawal more seriously than ever before. As has been said, there are at present opportunities for seizing price leadership that did not exist in more stable circumstances.

These measures are the more feasible because not only the customer but also the salesman has lost some orientation as far as price is concerned. Salesmen will therefore be less likely to adopt a negative attitude to increases, and by treating the company's price moves as a natural and inevitable result of current conditions may find their customers more receptive than they anticipated.

Success in obtaining higher prices enables a company to establish a pattern of tighter price discipline throughout the sales force which could prove valuable in future. It is, however, worth sounding a note of warning at this point. Tighter discipline may have saved companies over the last few months, but should pricing become a purely internal routine, policed by accountants, with no regard to the changes that may be happening in the market place, trouble lies ahead.

THE NEXT STAGE

The exact shape the next phase will assume is going to depend on the efforts of buyers to solve their present predicament, the extent of any business recession likely to take place and the degree to which inflation continues independently of these other factors. It seems to be generally agreed that inflation will continue at a fairly steep rate, impelled by the increasing cost of labour and the long-term world scarcity of raw materials. Some recession also seems inevitable, even if it is no more than the transient swing between quasi-boom and quasi-slump to which we have become accustomed over the past two decades. Economists may argue over the relative importance of these trends, but marketing men would be advised to go further than this and to consider carefully the effect of the inevitable reaction of buyers to a situation that has been tolerated partly because the onset of inflation coincided with a shortage of supplies and a lack of alternative sources. The disorientation arising from the present situation might well appear intolerable should conditions change, even if the change is no more than a slight tilting of the balance between supply and demand.

It is hard to believe that buyers will continue much longer to accept price increases uncritically. In the consumer field there are signs that customers are prepared to 'shop around' more keenly in search of bargains and that they are prepared to change buying habits to suit changing price levels. The switch from margarine to butter when butter prices were reduced and margarine began to cost as much or more is one instance of this. In industrial markets it may not always be so easy to make comparisons or to change purchasing patterns, but here too there are signs that pressure to buy now rather than risk a price increase is meeting with more resistance and that customers may be applying their own rules of thumb to what is or is not a reasonable increase. They may also decide to go out to tender more often and to insist on more competitive quotations before a decision is made.

This natural reaction from customers wishing to reorient themselves is likely to be amplified in conditions of shrinking demand, with the result that pricing will become rapidly more competitive. It is therefore likely that businesses will be faced with an almost unprecedented combination of inflated costs and tougher market conditions, and it seems possible that this change could come about very quickly. It may, in fact, already have started in some sectors of industry, with inevitable repercussions elsewhere. To produce an effective pricing policy in these circumstances will require:

- *Better understanding of the buyer/seller interface.*
  It is clear that price competition is strongest when a customer is buying an article he knows and has brought previously. This condition, which has been called the 'straight rebuy',[4] is the nearest approximation to the economist's model of pure competition. If it is desired to avoid a situation which allows the buyer to dictate his terms, it is better to attempt to change the straight rebuy to either a modified rebuy or a new buy altogether. This lays stress on product differentiation as a means of justifying higher price. In industrial marketing the tendency is already to compete on grounds other than price if at all possible, but in future this will require a greater degree of competence and imagination if it is to be successful. In other words, companies will have not only to talk about professional selling but also to practise it at all levels. The cost of enhanced promotional activity will have to be balanced against loss of profit from attempting to compete on price alone. It is therefore likely that marketing will resume the place in policy-making which it has tended to forfeit in the early stages of inflation. It should go without saying that product quality, delivery and after-sales service will have to match the

promotional effort made, and here too marketing has an important advisory role to play.

- *Better intelligence as far as market pricing is concerned.*
The research findings quoted previously have indicated that there may be considerable scope for error in a company's appreciation of its pricing structure relative to competition. In the past the sources of information on competitive prices and price acceptability have been primarily the sales force and internal sales staff. Very little formal investigation has been made into price acceptability, and this may be because research in this field is not easy. Research in inflationary times, when quick results are required if the information is to be of any use at all, poses very considerable problems. New techniques have to be developed, and the most promising approach would seem to lie in test marketing of a kind that will enable questions to be asked and answered more rapidly than has been customary. Pricing research may prove to be an opportunity area for the currently depressed market research industry, but few clients will be able to afford to wait three months for an answer, so conventional studies will be of little use and assistance with in-company test marketing might be a better proposition.

- *Maintenance of discipline with flexibility*
With the reservations already made on the sales force as a source of general pricing information it will pay nevertheless to listen to the salesman attempting to fine-tune his offer and to guide him in the best tactics in given situations. Too rigid a discipline can lose orders; too loose a control will lead to profit erosion. Rigidity may still pay dividends on one point, and that is in terms of sale, escalation clauses and similar anti-inflation devices. These will need to be maintained so long as the exact rate of inflation remains unpredictable.

- *Use of alternative methods for effecting price changes.*
It may be worth while exploring other means of altering prices, for example by changing the product specification or by the inclusion or omission of 'extras'. These tactics have already been widely employed in the automobile industry, but they do not seem to have found much favour elsewhere. They naturally serve to make direct price comparisons more difficult.

Undoubtedly scope exists for a wider use of such methods and there may well be areas where they are unlikely to cause an unfavourable customer reaction. They could, however, prove counter-productive in situations where a straight rebuy is made at fairly regular intervals. Furthermore, they are difficult and costly to administer compared with a simple price increase. The cost of making a physical change, including design, tooling and documentation, is the most obvious deterrent, but even changing sales literature can take time and absorb considerable expense. Both the Trade Descriptions Act and normal commercial practice make it essential that potential buyers are not misled by out-of-date information.

Apart from studying more oblique ways of increasing price it may be worth considering means of reducing price, other than by a straight reduction to list price, if a larger market share is sought at minimum additional cost and with minimum risk of retaliation. Time-honoured methods include 'loss leaders', special offers for a limited period, and 'package deals'. These have the advantage of flexibility and do not commit the company to a permanent reduction. As has been noted, there appears to be ample scope for the exercise of imagination in the application of discounts and in the promotional use made of price. Nevertheless, whatever the reaction of customers to such offers, the likely reaction of competitors will require close attention.

- *Better communication with competitors.*

It is clear that when tougher market conditions are combined with continuing inflation not all competitors are going to survive. There is, however, a danger that unless great care is taken in pricing decisions the more efficient companies will be dragged down with those which deserve to fail. Conditions of rising costs and shrinking demand argue for an increase in price along with a cut-back in production. This, however, can rarely be phased with any great accuracy, and where over-production occurs some competitors are likely to seek a larger market share to absorb the surplus. A price war may follow, to the detriment of all participants.

Just occasionally inflation may offer the opportunity of winning such a war by eliminating competitors known to be in serious financial difficulty, but that is a game for companies with deep pockets and strong nerves. Most others show far too deeply rooted a conservatism on matters of price to want to start a war. For them a price war is more of a threat than an opportunity. They have therefore to make sure that competitors at least understand the company's position, so that war is not provoked, as is so often the case, through ignorance. No collusion is involved in making plain the company's policy on price increases, discounts, special offers and similar matters. If, for example, an offer is of limited duration in order to clear stocks, and competitors know this, they can temper their reactions accordingly. Communication between competitors needs in many cases to be improved, and a fair measure of trust engendered between rival directors for this to be possible. Where it is possible—normally in fairly compact, oligopolistic type industries—the effort may be worthwhile, just as in international diplomacy the 'summit' meeting is of some use in making clear the intentions of the participants.

- *A more discerning measurement of results.*
  Table 6.4 indicates that for industrial companies the normal method of measuring the results of pricing decisions is a simple comparison of sales volume with that for similar periods in the past. It is clear that to navigate the tricky straits between inflation and recession a better guidance system will be required. Some of the techniques that might be employed are listed in Table 6.4 and may already be used much more frequently in consumer marketing. As well as these the number of orders for different categories of customer, the frequency of repeat orders and the creation of detailed industry statistics showing units sold as well as sales value are among the measures that might be employed.

Table 6.4 Method of Measuring Results of Pricing Decisions

Formal market investigation	14
Studying market shares from available statistics	32
Comparing sales results with those for comparable periods	73
Test marketing in a limited area	—
Other methods	7
Not stated	7

Figures shown are percentages (base 220)

To use the techniques described here effectively will demand better, and quicker, marketing decisions than were necessary either in pre-inflationary times or in the earlier stages of inflation. The only way in which quick decisions can be made on sound information, rather than hunch, is for such information to be continuously available. Even then companies will have to appreciate the risk values of the decisions to be taken and to use marketing expertise correctly, not as a panacea for all ills but as a guide to the course most likely to produce profit in a highly competitive situation. There is every danger that, if the need for all this is not foreseen and action taken in good time, the next stage will be characterised by tension between inflation-conscious accountants and salesmen demanding price cuts in the face of a hardening attitude on the part of increasingly cost-conscious customers. If timely action is taken, however, and prices are fixed on the basis of improved market information, companies will be able to reap the rewards of a more professional sales approach. This, combined with other measures not directly related to pricing, for example the co-ordination of marketing planning and production cut-back, the selection of those longer-term developments which can most profitably be abandoned or the identification of fresh opportunity areas, is a major contribution that marketing can make towards survival in the next phase of inflation.

NOTES AND REFERENCES

1. B. Atkin and R. Skinner, *How British Industry Prices*, Industrial Market Research Limited (London, 1975).
2. B. Atkin and R. Skinner, *op. cit.* This report relates to a survey which took place in 1974 when the nature of the present situation had already become apparent. The survey was, however, directed specifically to established practices and it was possible to obtain a clear picture of pre-inflationary thinking, as well as an indication of the problems then being encountered as a result of the onset of inflation.
3. B. Atkin and R. Skinner, *op. cit.*
4. P. J. Robinson, C. W. Faris and Y. Wind, *Industrial Buying and Creative Marketing*, Allyn & Bacon (Boston, Mass., 1967).

CHAPTER 7

Inflation and the Investment Decision

J. R. Franks and J. E. Broyles

The objective in this chapter is to discuss some of the implications of changes in the rate of inflation on the profitability of capital investment. We show that, under some very restrictive assumptions, changes in the rate of inflation should not affect the profitability of capital investment. However, the relaxation of some of the more unrealistic assumptions significantly alter our conclusions. Progressive income taxes and other income effects (discussed in the second section), and corporation taxes levied on nominal profits and stock gains (discussed in the third section) affect the profitability of capital investment in both nominal and real terms. Furthermore, increases in uncertainty concerning future changes in the rate of inflation can increase the costs of finance for capital investment, as discussed in the fourth section. In the fifth section we demonstrate that lags in price increases to recover costs, possibly resulting from price controls, can significantly alter returns from capital investment. Finally, we make some comments on the controversy over stock gains, concluding among other things that companies cannot benefit in real terms from after-tax stock gains unless the rate of gain is somewhat greater than the general rate of inflation.

RISKS, REQUIRED RATES OF RETURN AND INFLATION

On the basis of a simple model and with a very restrictive set of assumptions, one can show that a change in the rate of inflation would not alter the real returns on an investment. The model, based on the assumptions of an efficient market, states that the expected rate of return on a security is equal to the risk-free rate of return (e.g. an appropriate Treasury Bill rate) plus a premium for risk. This risk premium is a function of the asset's risk relative to that of the economy. In principle the model applies to the evaluation of capital projects as well as to marketable securities. The required rate of return for a project is equal to the risk-free rate of interest plus a risk premium, which is a function of the sensitivity of a project's returns in relation to changes in the economy. That is,

$$E(R_j) = R_F + \text{Risk Premium} \qquad (j = 1, 2, \ldots, J) \qquad (1)$$

where:

$E(R_j)$ = Required Rate of Return on the project j or its cost of capital

R_F = Risk-free Rate of Interest

The risk-free rate of interest reflects the anticipated rate of inflation, and any changes in that rate of inflation are assumed to be reflected fully and speedily in interest rates. Clearly, if interest rates do not reflect anticipated rates, commodity markets may be in some sense inefficient. If the anticipated rate of inflation is greater than the interest rate for the period, individuals would borrow funds and purchase commodities until either interest rates rose or anticipated price increases altered. Conversely, if interest rates are greater than anticipated relative price increases, the commodities would be sold short. The proposition that interest rates reflect anticipated rates of inflation was propounded by Irving Fisher, and is known as the 'Fisher Effect'.[1]

Thus the risk-free rate for a period when the real rate of interest is represented by r and the expected rate of inflation is g would be given by

$$R_f = (1 + r)(1 + g) - 1 \qquad (2)$$

The Fisher Effect is often used as a basis for the assertion that a change in the anticipated rate of inflation should have no effect on the profitability of capital investment.

Under the restrictive set of assumptions one can show that changes in the rate of inflation would not affect project profitability. We shall use Net Present Value (NPV) as an indicator of the profitability of capital investment:

$$\text{NPV} = \sum_{t=0}^{T} C_{jt}/(1 + R_j)^t \qquad (j = 1, 2, \ldots, J) \qquad (3)$$

where C_{jt} is the expected net incremental cash flow from project j at the end of period t and R_j is the required rate of return for assets in the same risk class as project j. If we assume that the project relates solely to an economy characterised by perfectly competitive markets without progressive income taxes, corporation taxes, price controls or other similar interventions or influences, we have for a risk-free project,

$$\text{NPV} = \sum_{t=0}^{T} c_0 (1 + g)^t / \{(1 + r)(1 + g)\}^t \qquad (4)$$

where c and r represent cash flows and interest rates respectively in real terms and where we have employed equation (2) to represent the Fisher Effect. The above equation reduces to:

$$\text{NPV} = \sum_{t=0}^{T} c_0 / (1 + r)^t \qquad (5)$$

in which the rate of inflation g no longer appears.

Thus under our assumptions the profitability of a risk-free project is not affected by changes in the rate of inflation.

An implication of this simple model would be that a 10 per cent per annum discounted-cash-flow (DCF) rate of return on a project would increase to 16 per cent if the rate of inflation were to increase from zero to 6 per cent per annum. However, the increase in the rate of return on the project would be offset entirely by the corresponding increase in the required rate of return or cost of capital, given our assumptions.

The Fisher Effect has been the subject of empirical research, and many economists such as Mundell[2] have expressed doubt concerning its validity. Roll[3] in his review of the literature concludes that the case for Fisher's proposition is unproven. Research is difficult in this area since the expected rate of inflation must be estimated for both real and paper assets. Roll points out that there is a scarcity of 'real securities' and, therefore, of relevant price data. If Fisher's proposition should not be an accurate reflection of the effect of expected rates of inflation on required rates of return, then there would be no obvious reason to suppose that the profitability of capital investments could remain unchanged by changes in the anticipated rates of inflation.

In the remainder of this chapter we show that, even if one were to accept the Fisher Effect as a useful approximation, the effect of income taxes, corporation taxes and, of course, price controls is to change the profitability of capital investment when there are changes in the rate of inflation.

INCOME EFFECTS

We have said that under various restrictive assumptions an unanticipated change in the rate of inflation in a perfectly competitive market should leave a project's real rate of return unaffected. This presumes that individuals do not suffer from 'money illusion', that is they react to changes in relative prices rather than changes in absolute prices. Thus a change in the general level of prices due to inflation should not of itself alter the allocation of expenditure between different goods and services. However, in a progressive income tax system inflation will change the marginal rates of tax paid by individuals if income for tax purposes is not adjusted for the rate of inflation. If inflation affects pre-tax incomes uniformly and if there is no money illusion, some individuals are still worse off as they move into higher tax brackets, and consumption patterns will be altered. The resulting shifts in demand for different services will have differing effects on project revenues depending on the price elasticities of product inputs and outputs.

An income effect may also be present if some consumer groups such as pensioners live on fixed incomes that are unrelated, or react slowly, to changes in the rate of inflation. Such forms of income redistribution which take place as a consequence of a change in the rate of inflation will alter the demand pattern for goods and services and, therefore, affect the revenues of capital investments in real terms. How strong the redistribution effects may be will depend upon the extent to which they are anticipated and effectively taken into account by different economic groups in establishing relative prices.

CORPORATION TAX, STOCKHOLDING AND PROJECT PROFITABILITY

Our analysis based on assumptions of a perfectly competitive market did not consider the effect that stock appreciation may have on the real returns for a project. However, the taxation of company profits is based upon monetary gains rather than real gains. Also, stock is normally valued on first-in-first-out (FIFO) basis in the UK. This method of taxing stock gains has given rise to controversy, since some commentators have suggested that stock gains are not real gains and should not therefore be taxed. A simple example illustrates the controversy.

		Period 1	*Period 2*
Purchases	100 units	£100	£120
Sales	100 units		£120

Profit and Loss A/C for Period 2

	£
Sales	120
Purchases	100
Profit	20
Tax (50%)	10
Profit After Tax	10

In the above example the reported profit for tax purposes is £20 and the tax payable is £10. However, if the firm has to replace the stock, which now costs £120 for 100 units, the firm has a cash-flow loss represented by the 'tax leakage' on the stock gain. Alternatively, if the tax system had been based on the last-in-first-out system (LIFO), the profit for tax purposes during the period would have been zero.

	£
Purchases	120
Sales	120
Profit	0

Under LIFO a tax on the stock gain is paid only when the stock ceases to be replaced. In this section we shall try to clarify these arguments and demonstrate their importance in the investment decision.

In the above example, under FIFO the firm has made a 10 per cent return on its investment after tax. The firm can either sell the stock for £100 in period 1 or wait and sell it at the end of period 2 at an expected nominal profit of 10 per cent. If the after-tax cost of finance should be less than 10 per cent, then the firm would find it attractive to hold stock, make nominal profits and pay corporation tax on these profits.

If inflation takes place at the expected rate and stock costs rise at the same rate, the firm would make the expected rate of return on its equity. Clearly the stock gains are a part of expected trading profit and should not be described as 'unreal'. The firm is aware of the prospective tax payment on stock gains when the investment in stock is undertaken. Provided that the gain is expected, the investment is made only if it is expected to be profitable after taxes. In this sense increases in the rate of inflation are only a threat to the profitability of an investment when the change is not expected. By definition an investment's profitability cannot be affected by subsequent changes in the rate of inflation if these changes have been taken into account in the original investment decision.

The previous analysis is not to be construed as implying that the FIFO-based tax system does not discriminate against stock-intensive investments during inflationary periods. However, we cannot argue that stock profits are unreal profits on the basis that stocks must be replaced. Stocks would not be replaced if firms did not find it profitable to do so.

Let us now examine and quantify the discriminatory effect of the FIFO system. We have already argued that inflation and stock gains which were expected do not change the project's profitability, but unanticipated increases in taxes payable due to unexpected inflation and consequent stock gains are a source of danger to corporate profitability. Although in the previous example we assumed that a company need not replace its stock if it were not profitable to do so, one recognises that a minimum stock of raw materials and of work in progress is required to keep most manufacturing processes going. Thus for much of manufacturing industry the level of stock becomes relatively insensitive to changes in the rate of inflation and interest rates. Capital projects in manufacturing industry need not be undertaken if they are seen to be unprofitable given expected rates of inflation. Consequently, corporate taxation under the FIFO method of assessment should tend to discourage capital investment by manufacturers in stock-intensive projects. Although the adverse effect of taxation on stock appreciation may not be sufficient to justify abandonment of an existing project, project profitability and company liquidity can be affected adversely by these taxes when the rate of inflation exceeds the rate which had been expected. Liquidity is affected adversely because taxes on stock gains are incurred concurrently with the reported gains but the cash flows are not realised until the stocks are no longer required to keep the project going.

The key to the analysis of the profitability of capital investment lies in the potential for reinvestment of cash flows generated by the project. If the realisation of the actual stock gains must be delayed until the project is abandoned, then the stock gain eventually to be realised cannot restore the lost reinvestment opportunities in the meantime. These reinvestment effects which make the timing of cash flows critical to the profitability of capital investment are automatically taken into account in discounted-cash-flow analyses. For this reason any discussion concerning the effect of changes in the rate of inflation on the profitability of capital investment should be argued in terms of discounted-cash-flow and net-present-value profitability.

In another paper[4] we have analysed the present-value effect of the corporation tax on stock gains. In order to find the relative effect we divided the present value of taxes on stock gains by the present value of all other cash flows (excluding capital expenditures) which would have been received if the project had been able to operate without any stock. In this way we were able to analyse the effect of carrying stock in an inflationary environment in which stock gains are taxed under the FIFO method of assessment.

Table 7.1 summarises our findings for four combinations of stockholding periods and rates of inflation assuming a profit margin of 10 per cent and corporation tax at 50 per cent. The table indicates the magnitude of the present value of the tax leakage on stock gains as a percentage of the present value of positive cash flows for the same project but without stock. The table therefore treats the unrealised stock gain as being postponed indefinitely.

Table 7.1 Present Value of Tax Leakage as a Percentage of the Present Value of the Same Project but Without Stock

	$l=2$ months	$l=4$ months
$g=2\%$	− 3·3%	− 6·6%
$g=12\%$	− 20%	− 40%

where: g — represents the unanticipated rate of inflation when the expected rate was zero

l — represents the stockholding period

Assumes: Corporation tax = 50%

Profit margin is 10%

If the expected rate of inflation is equal to zero but inflation rises to 2 per cent, the loss in present value is 3·3 per cent if the stockholding period is only two months; but the loss increases to 6·6 per cent if the stockholding period is four months. Alternatively, if the annual rate of inflation turns out to be 12 per cent, the loss of present value will be 40 per cent if the stockholding period is four months.

In the example represented in Table 7·1 we have assumed a profit margin of 10 per cent on each unit sold. Clearly, as operating margins increase, the tax leakage as a proportion of total profit decreases. The proportion will also change as a result of changes in the stockholding period, the tax rate and costs of finance, as well as a result of unexpected changes in inflation. With regard to changes in stockholding period and prices management often has very limited room for manoeuvre. The optimum stockholding period is relatively inelastic with respect to inflation for manufacturing industry. However, attempts by management to minimise the impact of corporation tax on stock gains by increasing profit margins may be blocked by Government price and profit margin controls.

At this point we have assumed that stock gains do not exceed the rate of inflation. If the stock gain is substantially in excess of the change in the rate of inflation (and the interest costs), then the project's real profitability can actually increase after corporate taxes. Of course the problem is symmetrical when unanticipated reductions in the rate of inflation result in stock losses: under these circumstances stock-intensive projects gain in profitability.

In the preceding analysis we have examined changes in the rate of inflation on an individual project's profitability. We have concluded that expected changes in inflation and stock gains are already reflected in the expected profitability of a project. However, this does not mean that the FIFO method of taxation is not discriminatory compared to the LIFO method. Indeed, *ceteris paribus*, FIFO as compared with LIFO will lead to a lower level of investment in stock-intensive projects in an inflationary environment. This reallocation of resources will increase as the expected rate of inflation increases.

How important are stock gains? M. A. King in a recent paper[5] suggests that stock appreciation constituted a substantial proportion of total corporate profits (after taxes and after a provision for capital consumption). We have reproduced in Table 7.2 his data for the period 1965–73.

It is impossible to estimate how large a proportion of these stock gains had been expected when capital investments were undertaken. If the stock gains were expected, then companies have not reaped unexpected profits from inflation. If the gains had not been expected, we still cannot say *a priori* that companies are better off in net-present-value profitability terms. King states that 'from 1970 to 1973 the price index of stocks in manufacturing rose by 35·7 per cent as compared to a rise of 25·3 per cent

Table 7.2 Profits in UK Manufacturing 1965–73 (£m)

	Post-tax profits less stock appreciation and capital consumption	*Stock appreciation*
1965	1987	182
1966	1677	185
1967	1746	90
1968	1743	332
1969	1573	390
1970	1405	683
1971	1488	625
1972	1810	745
1973	2064	1636

Sources: Central Statistical Office and *Blue Book*.

in the consumer price index'. He concludes therefore that real gains were made from stock appreciation. One can question this conclusion since King has not allowed for tax, and we have already shown that the FIFO method of taxation implies that the rate of stock gains must be greater than the inflation rate just to leave the firm no worse off in real terms after tax.

IMPLICATIONS OF INFLATION ON A PROJECT'S RISK PREMIUM

The risk premium component of the project's discount rate reflects its risk relative to the market for risky assets. Such a premium will reflect the variance in rates of inflation. Referring to equation (1), as uncertainty increases concerning the anticipated rate of inflation, the risk premium on the market increases. If the cash flows for a risky project are positively correlated with the market, the project's required rate of return will increase as a result of increased uncertainty concerning future rates of inflation.

We have already shown that under certain circumstances stock-intensive projects may be affected more than the average project in the market from unexpected changes in the rate of inflation. Thus the increase in project risk due to an increase in uncertainty concerning future rates of inflation may be correspondingly greater for stock-intensive projects than for projects which require little or no stock.

THE EFFECTS OF DIFFERENTIAL COST AND PRICE INCREASES AND LAGS IN COST RECOVERY

The project's discount rate has been discussed in money or nominal terms; it is therefore necessary that the forecasts of costs and revenues and the resulting forecasts of project's cash flows be in monetary terms. Up to this point we have discussed the anticipated rate of inflation for the economy. However, the costs and revenues of one industry may be rising at a different rate from that of inflation generally. Furthermore, costs and prices for the industry may also be rising at different rates. The fact that costs and revenues are rising at different rates is due to the demand and supply for the various inputs and outputs and cannot necessarily be ascribed to changes in the general level of prices.

Notwithstanding this, the effect of leads and lags is still present and may alter the project's returns. If we assume that there is cost inflation, manufacturers may delay in passing on increases. However, eventually manufacturers will realise the impact on profitability and cash flow and may anticipate cost increases and raise prices accordingly: their ability to do so will depend upon competitive conditions. Frequently leads and lags will be present and will affect profitability. We do not make a distinction here between the origins or causes of the inflation, although Hicks has stated[6] that 'profits tend to rise faster than other costs in demand inflations and lag behind during wage inflations'. At higher rates of inflation the Government may control the prices of labour in some markets but not in others while, for example, interest rates may be kept below the market rate. Such interference will affect project profitability in money terms and in real terms. Management often makes the mistaken assumption that costs and revenues rise at the same rate and simultaneously. In this section we shall examine implications of taking such differences into account in the appraisal of a project.

In our first case[7] we shall examine a project with a life of five years. Operating costs include both labour and materials in the ratio of 1:1. In addition, we specify the ratio of operating costs to capital costs. In Table 7.3 we assume that the anticipated rate of inflation is 10 per cent and the required rate of return (risk-adjusted) is 15 per cent. We alter labour costs by increments of 1 per cent, and we examine the effects on two projects

Table 7.3 Impact on DCF Returns of Different Cost and Revenue Changes

Annual rate of increase		DCF returns with ratios of annual operating costs to capital costs of:	
Revenue and material	*Labour*	*1:1*	*2:1*
6%	6%	16·5%	16·5%
6%	7%	14·5%	12·0%
6%	8%	12·0%	7·0%
6%	9%	10·0%	1·0%

Note: 100 per cent first-year capital allowance is assumed to operate.

with different ratios of operating costs to capital costs. Clearly, if any part of operating costs is rising at a faster rate than prices, the impact will increase as the ratio of operating costs (labour and material) increases. The results in the table show that small changes in one component of operating costs will significantly affect the DCF returns. Such a differential may arise because of Government controls, which may reduce an industry's profitability, or it may occur at any rate of inflation due to demand and supply changes for the various factors of production.

In Table 7.4 we have results for a similar project where all costs and revenues are rising at the same rate but where labour cost increases are not recovered until one year after they are incurred.

Table 7.4 Impact of a Delay in Recovering Cost Increases by One Year

Annual increase in costs	DCF returns with ratio of annual operating costs to capital costs of:	
	1:1	*2:1*
6%	9·5%	4·6%
9%	9·1%	1·3%
12%	8·5%	0
15%	7·9%	0

Note: A 100 per cent first-year capital allowance is assumed to operate.

One can arrive at a number of conclusions from the results in Tables 7.3 and 7.4:

- Small changes in costs and revenue can significantly affect investment profitability. The effect increases as the ratio of operating costs to capital costs increases.
- Delays in recovering costs can be more damaging than the failure to recover costs entirely if the delay is recurrent.
- To the extent that the Prices Commission has been successful in delaying the recovery of cost increases by companies, it has been responsible in part for a loss in corporate profitability and the recent collapse of share prices.

There are three implications for management action here. Obviously pressure on the Government to abolish price control is important. However, given the fact that there are price controls, the rapid monitoring of costs in order to speed the submission of proposed price increases to the Prices Commission is essential. In evaluating investments, account must be taken of the effects of changes in the rate of inflation on revenues and costs and of any delays in passing increased costs on to the customer. Such delays may be caused by the firm's own inability to make frequent price adjustments. This inability may result from a tardy or inflexible financial control system and from the rapidity of unanticipated changes in the rate of inflation. Of course, the Prices Commission, to say nothing of customers, may delay the implementation of proposed price increases.

In our analysis we have always discussed returns and costs of finance in monetary terms. We believe that analysis in monetary terms works better in practice than the often futile attempts by managers to convert cash flows correctly into real terms. In monetary terms management can more easily estimate differential rates of change and time lags in cost and revenues, and compute the associated corporation taxes, which are levied in monetary terms rather than in real terms. Also analysis in real terms may require discounting cash flows at very low or even negative rates. It is difficult to convince management of negative real required rates of return in practice.

INFLATION AND FINANCIAL CONTROL

Rapidly changing rates of inflation and the uncertainty of future rates have made it increasingly difficult to monitor and forecast costs and revenues, evaluate capital investment and compare performance. Usually the financial control system of the firm has not been designed to provide information to management with the frequency and timeliness necessary. Since the redistribution effects of inflation coupled with Government intervention appear so great, the company has little choice but to produce a cost-control system that monitors and updates at frequent intervals. Investment projects may have to be evaluated more frequently as they progress, as cost and revenue forecasts become outdated; and costs of capital must be revised as interest rates change. A high rate of inflation does not require a new theory of financial control: it merely requires the system to be faster and more flexible, and management to understand the problems before they are submerged by them.

CONCLUSIONS

Assuming perfectly competitive markets, we have shown that under certain conditions a change in the anticipated rate of inflation may affect corporate profitability in real terms, for example through the income effect of a progressive tax system. The effect may be reflected in a change in revenues (depending on the price elasticities of demand and supply) and in a change in the risk of an asset relative to other assets. We also found that a corporation tax system based on the FIFO stock valuation method can reduce profitability in real terms by the amount of tax leakage on stock gains. Management's ability to restore profitability through price increases will depend upon the competitive structure of the market for its products. However, since prices on products requiring investment in stock have to increase at a greater rate than the prices of other goods or services requiring less stock, it would be surprising if real profitability were unaffected.

During 1974, with the rapid increase in commodity prices, certain firms in the UK economy made unexpected after-tax stock gains that greatly exceeded the change in the general rate of inflation and interest rates. Clearly such gains, if sufficiently large, can add to a company's real profitability. It may be argued that if the stock must be replaced the company cannot be better off. We see no necessity to distinguish between realised and unrealised real gains and would merely point out that the criterion for an increase in profitability rests on an increase in the net present value of the firm. It is entirely consistent to claim that the value of a firm's assets has increased; but since it is profitable to keep in business and maintain the present level of activity, the gains remain unrealised; and, consequently, the cash flow of the firm in that particular year does not benefit. Such real gains should be treated by both Government and unions as once-and-for-all gains that cannot necessarily be repeated. Thus trade unions should realise that, although they may wish to increase wage demands as a result of such exceptional gains, they should not expect more than an annuity equivalent to some proportion of real stock gain after corporation taxes.

It is clear from our analysis that the FIFO method of taxation can be discriminatory under inflationary conditions. If the Government wishes to remove this discrimination, it should consider either a change to the LIFO system for fiscal purposes or a reduction in the tax on stock profits. The other possibility is to tax only those stock gains in excess of the rate of inflation.[8] Acceptance of these proposals would clearly imply similar treatment of stock losses, and it is not unimportant at which point in the trade cycle such a tax change should take place.

Given King's analysis on corporate profits, it appears that stocks have made an increasing contribution to total profits, and therefore the current system of taxing stock profits could have borne very heavily on particular sectors. It is possible that stock gains have been greater than the rate of inflation, but it must be stressed that this must always be the case if firms taxed under FIFO are not to be worse off. We believe that the effects which we have described can adversely affect companies, particularly in the manufacturing sector, and reduce capital investment under inflationary conditions, especially when that inflation is unexpected.

In this chapter we have been concerned with the effects of changes in the rate of inflation on the profitability of capital investment. We have employed a discounted-cash-flow profitability analysis and endeavoured to show that the assumptions employed can affect one's conclusions. We suggest that an analysis of this nature should be employed by those who wish to discuss, for example, the implications of inflation accounting or of fiscal changes with regard to the taxing of stock gains.

NOTES AND REFERENCES

1. Irving Fisher, *The Theory of Interest*, Macmillan (New York, 1930).
2. Robert Mundell, 'Inflation and Real Interest', *Journal of Political Economy*, June 1963.
3. R. Roll, 'Interest Rates on Monetary Assets and Commodity Price Index Changes', *Journal of Finance*, May 1972, pp. 251–78.
4. J. E. Broyles and J. R. Franks, 'Some Implications of Change in the Rate of Inflation for Capital Investment', unpublished paper, London Graduate School of Business Studies.
5. M. A. King, 'The United Kingdom Profits Crisis: Myth or Reality?', *The Economic Journal*, March 1975.
6. J. R. Hicks, 'Inflation and Interest Rates', *Banca Nazionale del Lavoro* (1974).
7. *See* J. R. Franks and H. H. Scholefield, *Corporate Financial Management*, Gower Press (London, 1974), Chapter 7.
8. M. A. King, *op. cit.*

CHAPTER 8

Management Accounting under Conditions of Inflation

P. R. A. KIRKMAN

Accountants frequently suggest that one of the major reasons for business failure is the lack of financial advice. It is difficult to assess how true such generalisations are, but it is considered to be most important that in the difficult financial atmosphere of the mid-1970s all businessmen should have at least a superficial knowledge of finance and accounting. In addition, the advice of the fully qualified up-to-date accountant should prove invaluable on many occasions, not just in connection with past performance but also in the preparation of short-term and long-term plans.

In most cases the small businessman uses the services of an external practising accountant, primarily in connection with the accounting statements that are required for taxation purposes. Unfortunately, the historical accounts are frequently not used for any other purpose, and the accountant may not be asked for advice on future business plans. In these circumstances the accountant is acting in his traditional role as a supplier of historical accounting information, and no attempt is made to utilise his skills in the financial planning area.

In many medium-sized and large companies, however, accountants are employed in a full-time capacity, not just as providers of historical information but as most important contributors towards the overall planning system of the business organisation. This management accounting function is extremely important, especially in current inflationary conditions when it becomes increasingly difficult to survive without proper planning systems.

It is important to appreciate that most management accounting systems are based on records of past performance. In this chapter, therefore, a brief examination will be carried out initially of the way in which the accountant measures business performance. In current conditions of extreme inflation, conventional profit measurement methods are extremely unsatisfactory, and revised methods have been recommended by the UK accountancy bodies and a Government-appointed commitee of enquiry—the Sandilands Committee.[1] Historical accounting statements in any form are, however, of limited value, as nothing can be done to change past trading performance. The latter part of this chapter will therefore be concerned with financial planning systems. These systems should help considerably in the survival process, although they obviously cannot guarantee that the demand for the products that have been sold in the past will continue in the future.

THE MEASUREMENT OF BUSINESS PERFORMANCE

Business profit has traditionally been measured by means of a comparison between costs and revenue. This system was reasonably satisfactory when the purchasing power of money did not change significantly from one year to another, but in current conditions with inflation in the UK in excess of 20 per cent per annum there is naturally a very important difference between the purchasing power of the pound in, say, 1970 and 1975.

If therefore a private individual or a property company purchased buildings in 1970 for £10000 and sold them in 1975 for £18000, what significance can be attached to the conventional profit figure of £8000, especially if replacement buildings have to be purchased? Some businessmen would suggest that the figure of £8000 is of little value, but unfortunately our taxation and dividend systems are still largely tied to traditional methods of profit measurement.

The present profit measurement situation is therefore not really satisfactory in conditions of inflation, although there are obvious problems if attempts are made to measure profit in purchasing-power terms as opposed to conventional money terms. If we return to the property example, attempts could be made to measure the change in the purchasing power of the pound between the date of purchase in 1970 and the date of sale in 1975. The best known UK price indicator, the index of retail prices, might show that the general level of prices for goods and services had increased by 50 per cent in the period under consideration. In this case it might be suggested that the revised profit figure should be £3000, i.e. the £18000 sale price less an adjusted purchase price of £15000 (£10000 + 50 per cent).

This is basically the suggestion of the UK accountancy bodies as contained in a provisional statement issued in May 1974, and this approach has been supported by accountants in several other countries. Such a system of accounting is generally described in the UK as current purchasing power (CPP) accounting, and if the suggestions are accepted supplementary accounting statements based on the current purchasing power of the local unit of currency will be provided by corporations in addition to conventional accounting information. At first glance these proposals might appear to be attractive to the businessman, but it is debatable whether they provide any great assistance in the process of survival.

It would almost certainly be suggested by advocates of CPP accounting that the revised profit figure of £3000 is more realistic than the conventional profit figure of £8000. Admittedly it does provide some valuable information regarding the comparative increase in property values as compared with general prices, but it does not take into account the cost of replacement buildings. This type of system is therefore primarily concerned with the general purchasing power of money, and little or no attention is given to the price that will have to be paid for a replacement asset.

In the property example that has already been considered the advocate of a rather different system of accounting—current replacement cost (CRC) accounting—might suggest that no profit at all has been made, if a very similar replacement property is being purchased in the same area at about the same price. Indeed, if there are substantial buying and selling expenses, it might be suggested that a loss has been made. The private individual who moves to another part of the country where house prices are significantly cheaper may gain, but it is just as likely that he will make a move into a more expensive area.

The end result under the CRC accounting system, therefore, may be a profit figure that is related much more closely to available cash resources than under a conventional or a CPP accounting system. In commerce and industry, however, the typical business organisation may sell thousands of items every day, and it would be extremely difficult to calculate the immediate cost of replacing goods, especially in the manufacturing organisation where many processes are involved. In addition, technological developments frequently lead to a situation where identical replacement goods are no longer available.

In 1974 over forty UK companies produced supplementary accounting statements adjusted for changes in the general purchasing power of money. One of the leaders in these developments has been the large retail group Currys Limited. In their 1973 Annual Report and Accounts supplementary inflation-adjusted information was published for the first time together with the following additional comments for shareholders:

> The group profit unappropriated on a current purchasing power basis is £515 000 less than the profit on a historical basis. This difference can be illustrated in very basic form by a simple analogy. Imagine a street trader who purchases a refrigerator for £30. By the end of the week he sells it for £40. He now replenishes his stock by purchasing another refrigerator. He finds, however, that because of inflation he must now pay £32. The question to be asked is: 'How much profit has the trader made?' An accountant using the traditional historical cost basis will say he has made: £40 (selling price) less £30 (cost price) = £10 profit. The trader, however, looks at the pound notes in his pocket available for spending, i.e. £40 (selling price) less £32 (replacement cost) = £8 profit. On this basis his profit available for distribution is reduced by £2. Similarly Currys Limited have a smaller sum available for distribution than that shown by historical cost accounting.

It will be noted that in this example pound notes available for spending are equated with profit. Unfortunately, many businessmen in a similar situation are not aware of the limitations of conventional accounting statements, and as a result the whole of the historical profit after taxation may be regarded as available for distribution.

In one important respect, however, the example provided by Currys Limited is not a satisfactory illustration of CPP accounting as such a system does not generally involve the use of replacement costs. The profit figure under the two systems of inflation accounting would only be the same if general prices and refrigerator prices had increased in exactly the same way. As general prices are unlikely to have increased by $6\frac{2}{3}$ per cent ($\frac{2}{30} \times 100$) in a week it would seem that in this particular example CPP accounting would show a rather higher profit than CRC accounting. In correspondence on this matter the managing director of Currys stressed that the example given was an attempt 'to provide an explanation that a small investor (the vicar's wife, for example) might understand'. In the 1974 accounts, however, the example provided in the previous year's accounts was omitted. This illustrates the great difficulty of explaining general price-level adjustments in simple language.

The latest inflation-adjusted accounts of the Currys organisation are reproduced in Table 8.1. From the information provided for the year ended 30 January 1975 it will be seen that the group profit available after taxation—usually described as earnings—was £3096000 using conventional accounting methods as opposed to £1632000 under the CPP system of inflation accounting. Expressed in earnings per share there was a fall from 13·9p to 7·6p, a reduction of over 45 per cent.

Stockholding Gains

The make-up of the reduction in earnings is provided in a schedule attached to the inflation-adjusted accounts (*see* Table 8.2, p. 134). From this it will be seen that the major adjustment factor was related to stock values, i.e. £2442000. The opening stock valuation in a retail company such as Currys will usually be a mixture of costs incurred in the last few months of the previous financial year. Under the CPP accounting system stock figures are 'updated' to end of year purchasing-power terms with the aid of the retail prices index (RPI). It will be seen from the accounts that the RPI increased by 19·9 per cent during the latest financial year. The most controversial aspect of these proposals is obviously related to the fact that purchase costs may move in a very different way from the RPI. It is extremely difficult for the external analyst to assess whether profit adjustments would have been similar if sales had been matched against replacement costs. An assessment of the profit figure using this approach should not be too difficult to calculate internally in a retail organisation with a limited number of stock lines and high-quality stock records, but in a complex manufacturing organisation there could be many problems attached to this method.

There is, unfortunately, a considerable amount of misunderstanding regarding the precise nature and significance of stockholding gains. This type of gain can probably be most easily explained with the aid of a simple example. The Brown Garage Limited purchased petrol for £1000 shortly before the announcement of a substantial price increase. The petrol was sold for £1250 but replacement petrol cost £1100. In this case the conventional profit figure would be £250; this would be made up of genuine trading profit of £150 and a stockholding gain of £100. Several UK oil companies have recently included comments on this matter in their annual report and accounts; for instance, British Petroleum announced in mid-1974 that the profit for the first quarter of 1974 of £295·5 million included non-recurring stockholding gains of approximately £175 million.

In 1974 a considerable amount of pressure was put on the Government to provide some tax relief for business organisations on stockholding gains. Eventually in November of that year the Chancellor introduced some taxation concessions, and the allowances provided were extended in April 1975. At the present moment companies are allowed to reduce their profit for taxation purposes by the excess of the year's increase in the book value of stocks over 10 per cent of trading profit. This is inevitably a rather haphazard approach to the problem, but it has provided much needed liquidity relief for many UK commercial and industrial organisations.

As far as the businessman is concerned it is most important that he should appreciate the similarities and the differences between the CPP accounting adjustments for stock items and the taxation allowances that have now been introduced. In both cases it is accepted that business profit may be distorted because of the inclusion in profit of stockholding gains that come about primarily because of inflation and not because of trading activity. Under the CPP accounting system the profit reduction is calculated with the aid of a general price index. The CRC accounting system and the recently introduced tax allowances are, however, more closely related to stock price changes than general price changes, and the end result could be a very different profit figure, especially if there have been dramatic price increases, as with oil products, or even price decreases, as with wool and copper in 1974–5.

Depreciation

It will be noted, however, that there are a number of other important adjustment factors in Currys's accounts. Depreciation needs to be adjusted because the figure shown as a cost in business accounts is frequently based on asset costs of several years ago. For example, a machine was purchased for £2000 in 1970. It was expected to last five years and at the end of that time it will be worthless. Most companies spread the cost of a long-term

Table 8.1 Currys—Consolidated Profit and Loss Account—Year Ended 30th January 1975

		Historical basis			*Current Purchasing Power basis (CPP) (1975 pounds)*	
		1975 52 weeks £'000		*1974 53 weeks £'000*	*1975 52 weeks £'000*	*1974 53 weeks £'000*
Group Turnover		100578		86443	109597	109381
Group Trading Profit		6730		7767	5316	8605
Surplus on Sale of Properties		128		92	78	32
Group Profit before Taxation		6858		7859	5394	8573
Taxation		3762		3878	3762	4650
Group Profit Available after Taxation		3096		3981	1632	3923
Appropriated as follows:						
Inflation Reserve	1465		710		—	—
Dividends	812		748		813	898
		2277		1458		
Group Profit Unappropriated for year		819		2523	819	3025

Net Current Assets		14556		11362		15018		13913
Fixed Assets less Depreciation		14909		12497		25042		22823
		29465		23859		40060		36736
Less: Preference Shares	660		660		660		792	
Deferred Taxation	6766		3444		6766		4129	
		7426		4104		7426		4921
Total Equity Interest		22039		19755		32634		31815
Ratios								
Return on Equity Interest		14·6%		19·8%		5·4%		12·0%
Net Assets per Share		94·6p		84·1p		140·1p		135·8p

Note re CPP columns: The figures in the Current Purchasing Power basis columns were arrived at by converting the corresponding figures in the basis columns by reference to the changes in price indices between the dates of the original transactions and January 1975. As indicated the CPP figures for both 1975 and 1974 are measured in pounds of purchasing power at January 1975. The Retail Price Index at January 1975 was 119·9 and at January 1974 was 100·0 and the rate of inflation for the year was 19·9% (12·0%).

Table 8.2—Currys—Profit Reconciliation Statement

The following explanation was provided by Currys regarding the differences between the figures shown in the historical account and the current purchasing power statement:

		1975 *£'000*		*1974* *£'000*
Group Profit after Taxation and Dividends (Historical basis)		2284		3233
Adjustments to convert to Current Purchasing Power basis:				
Stocks	2442		843	
Additional charge based on restating the cost of Stocks at the beginning and end of the year in CPP pounds, thus taking the inflationary element out of the profit on the sale of Stocks.				
Depreciation	472		267	
Additional Depreciation based on cost of Fixed Assets measured in CPP pounds.				
Monetary Items	(1368)		(396)	
Net gain in purchasing power resulting from the effects of inflation on the Group's				

These are increased by the change in the index between the average date at which they occurred and the end of the year. This adjustment increases profit as sales exceed the costs included in this heading.

	1975		1974	
Surplus on Sale of Properties	50		119	
Reduction of Surplus measured by relating sales proceeds to costs in CPP pounds.	——		——	
Transfer to Inflation Reserve		1465		710
Group Profit Unappropriated (Current Purchasing Power pounds at end of 1975 and 1974 respectively)		819		2523
Adjustment required to update 1974 profit from 1974 pounds to 1975 pounds		—		502
Group Profit Unappropriated (CPP basis at January 1975)		819		3025

Note: The Preference Share Capital of £660386 at the beginning of the year is equivalent in purchasing power to £791803 at the end of the year (because inflation has been 19·9% during the year). As the Company's liability to the Preference Shareholders is fixed in money terms this liability has declined during the year in real terms from £791803 to £660386. This reduction of £131417 in the Company's obligation in CPP terms is included in the net gain on Monetary Items of £1368000 shown above.

asset in equal instalments over its expected lifetime. If this approach was adopted, £400 would be included as a cost in the profit and loss accounts for 1970, 1971, 1972, 1973 and 1974. In the 1974 accounts, therefore, depreciation based on 1970 price levels will be matched, together with other costs, against 1974 sales. The end result, if prices have changed significantly between 1970 and 1974 will be a distorted profit figure.

CPP accounting involves the use of a general price index to update pounds of past years into pounds of current purchasing power. In the case of a retail organisation like Currys the total depreciation adjustment may not be comparable with the adjustment for stocks. In a large manufacturing organisation, however, such as Imperial Chemical Industries Limited, the depreciation adjustment may be much greater than the comparable adjustment for stocks and work-in-progress because of the large amount of machinery employed in the organisation.

Once again there is a dispute about the appropriate adjustment method between the advocates of the two major methods of inflation accounting, as the supporter of CRC accounting would prefer to make adjustments with a number of specific asset price indices rather than one general index. The external analyst will have great difficulty in finding out what the differences between the two systems might be, but company management should be able to make at least a few enquiries to discover how specific fixed asset prices have changed, although technological developments will make comparisons very difficult in some areas of commerce and industry.

Net Monetary Liabilities

The other major adjustment in Currys's accounts is described as the 'net gain in purchasing power resulting from the effects of inflation on the Group's net monetary liabilities'. In this type of situation losses or gains may be made depending on the company's monetary policy. If there is an excess of monetary assets over monetary liabilities, for example, if a considerable amount of cash is held at the bank, there will generally be a loss since the purchasing power of the money held at the bank will decline because of inflation. On the other hand, the company that is in debt will gain because the purchasing power of amounts repaid will not be as great as it was at the time the debts were incurred.

The most controversial aspect of these proposals relates to long-term debt and preference shares. The UK accountancy bodies have suggested that in both cases purchasing-power gains should be calculated yearly, regardless of the date when repayment will take place. With the Currys preference shares, therefore, the £660 386 that was outstanding at the beginning of the latest financial year is the equivalent in purchasing-power terms of £791 803 at 30 January 1975. This results in a purchasing-power gain of £131 417, and this has been included in the overall monetary gain of £1 368 000, most of which probably relates to short-term items.

To many financial observers the inclusion in earnings of a purchasing-power gain on long-term monetary items is unacceptable. Some writers feel that these items are not company gains but are gains made by the ordinary shareholders at the expense of other providers of capital. The majority of businessmen who have examined this issue in depth would probably accept that a gain is made in the long term, but there is a strong feeling that gains of this nature should not be regarded as part of profit available for distrubition to shareholders. At the very least it would seem that the long-term gains should be dealt with separately as non-trading items and should be matched against interest charges, preference dividends, etc. The Sandilands Committee was opposed to the inclusion of these gains in distributed profit, although the UK accountancy bodies have argued that 'it is inconsistent to exclude such gains when profit has been debited with the cost of borrowing which must be assumed to reflect anticipation of inflation by the lender during the currency of the loan'.

The decision as to whether monetary gains should be included in earnings available for distribution to shareholders will obviously make a large difference to inflation-adjusted earnings figures. The London stockbrokers Phillips & Drew, working on external evidence, have suggested that overall earnings for 1974 for 116 leading UK companies would decrease by 10 per cent using the recommendations of the UK accountancy bodies. If, however, monetary gains were not regarded as part of profits available for distribution, revised overall earnings would probably fall by 55 per cent. Naturally many company chairmen would not be happy about a fall of this proportion, unless there were prospects of the taxation system being linked to the revised earnings figure. There would also be many problems about the size of dividend payments; in the case of Currys, for example, the amount available for distribution if all monetary gains were excluded would be £264 000 (£1 632 000 less £1 368 000) as opposed to actual dividend payments of £812 000. The end result so far as investors and the Stock Exchange were concerned might be disastrous!

Recommendations

The businessman should appreciate that at the present moment we are in a position where most people agree that conventional profit figures are unsatisfactory, but no completely satisfactory alternative method of accounting is available. To many people CPP accounting is an unsatisfactory compromise solution, but it is virtually ready for national implementation and over forty UK companies published supplementary information of this nature in 1974. On the other hand, CRC accounting is not acceptable at the present moment to the UK accountancy bodies for external reporting purposes, primarily because of the difficulties involved in estimating replacement costs in a period of rapid technological change.

This does not mean, however, that CRC accounting could not be used for internal management purposes.

It is suggested, therefore, that the businessman who wishes to survive under conditions of inflation should no longer attach any great value to conventional profit figures, although information of this nature will still have to be prepared to comply with company and taxation legislation. If realistic historical profit information is considered to be important for decision-making purposes it should, if possible, be prepared on CRC accounting lines with stock and depreciation items updated to current price levels. If CPP accounts have to be prepared for publication purposes there is no reason why further adjustments should not be made where there have been significant differences between general and specific price changes. For the non-quoted organisation there may be difficulties in the absence of a full-time accountant; it is hoped, however, that the external practising accountant will be prepared to co-operate in the provision of more meaningful data over and above the preparation of accounts for taxation purposes. Even if this is not feasible the enlightened businessman should be able to make an appropriate revision of his accounts based on price changes that have taken place in the stock and fixed asset areas.

Conventional profit or loss figures will obviously affect taxation commitments, and they will generally play a part in the determination of dividends and other withdrawals out of the business. Apart from these areas there are few internal decisions that should be significantly affected by past profit performance. Small businesses often base their costings and their prices on past performance, but these should if possible be linked to current and expected future performance, although such ideas might be disputed by the Prices Commission! Last but by no means least it is liquidity rather than profit which is now dominating the thoughts of most businessmen, although profits obviously cannot be ignored in the long term. In these circumstances cash budgeting and planning is essential, and most of the second part of this chapter will be concerned with these processes which are becoming increasingly important in the battle for survival.

FINANCIAL PLANNING

A proper financial planning system should be part of the survival kit of every business organisation. Financial plans can, of course, be short term or long term. In recent years most large UK companies have set up corporate planning departments which have been mainly concerned with long-term planning processes; the long term in this connection has generally been regarded as somewhere between three and seven years into the future.

Most small and medium-sized business organisations are, however, far more involved with short-term financial plans, which are primarily concerned with the current or the following financial year. The reasons for this are fairly obvious. First of all, long-term corporate planning is an expensive process and needs highly skilled staff. Secondly, our current extremely uncertain inflationary conditions have produced a situation where the emphasis is all too often on short-term survival, and any attempts to plan more than a year or two in advance are frequently regarded as a complete waste of time. In most cases the accountant would not accept this proposition, but it is an understandable viewpoint in current conditions.

In these circumstances the short-term budgeting process is probably more important than it has ever been before, with particular emphasis being placed on the cash flow part of the budgeting system. This is an important change from the profit-orientated budgeting system of a few years ago. This change has at least been partly caused by conventional methods of profit measurement which do not make satisfactory provision for increased replacement costs. In current inflationary conditions rapidly increasing raw material and fixed asset prices create constant cash-flow problems, even in those companies which appear to be extremely profitable. As a result the cash budget may be more important in the short term than profitability, although in the long term the businessman must aim for a satisfactory return on capital in order to produce positive net cash inflows.

Budgetary Control

Many books have been written on budgetary control[2] to help the businessman improve or install short-term planning and control systems. Most of these books were originally written when prices were rising at a rate of less than 5 per cent per annum. In current conditions, with inflation in excess of 20 per cent per annum, a situation has arisen in which realistic budgeting is more difficult than it has ever been before. At the same time, however, budgeting has become far more important, for without it the business organisation may not be able to survive. It is essential, therefore, that the businessman should understand budgeting systems. In particular he should appreciate that a system which was adequate five years ago may not be satisfactory today as inflation is having an increasing effect on budgeted costs and revenue.

Business budgets have traditionally been prepared in the UK for a full financial year, with the year being divided up into twelve monthly or thirteen 'four-weekly' periods. In many cases this approach has been adopted because of the system that is used for financial reporting purposes. In the last two or three years, however, many companies have had to revise or even abandon their budget for the latter part of the financial year because of dramatic increases in costs or even in selling prices. In current circumstances, therefore, it is debatable whether it is worthwhile preparing a budget in full for the whole of the financial year. Businessmen may well find that a detailed budget for, say, the first three or six months of the financial year, accompanied by an outline budget for the remainder of the year, is preferable to a detailed budget for the whole of the year which will almost inevitably have to be revised at a later date. The less detailed part of the budget will, of course, be finalised and produced in greater detail at a later stage in the year. The approach to this problem will obviously vary tremendously from one company to another as the degree of uncertainty can be so very different.

In most cases proper consultation with departmental heads will take place before budgets are finalised. This process of consultation may show significant variations from one company to another. Ideally, each departmental manager should be responsible for at least the intial preparation of his budget. In these circumstances it is most important that senior management should provide some general guidelines regarding budget preparation. In particular, departmental managers should be given some guidance on projected rates of inflation, as one manager might expect a future annual rate of 20 per cent whilst another may make no allowance for increased costs.

A number of different approaches have been used in this problem area; for example, managers responsible for departmental costs may be instructed:

a. To base their budgets on current costs;
b. to assume a future monthly inflation rate of, say, 2 per cent;
c. to make their own estimates of future costs;
d. to prepare a number of budgets based on different price levels.

Unfortunately, far too little guidance has been provided in this most difficult subject area, and managers are frequently blamed for cost increases which they are unable to control. If, as has already been suggested, detailed budgets are only prepared for a short period ahead, such as three months, it should be possible to keep a fairly close check on changing costs and price levels. The less detailed outline budget for the remainder of the year can then be updated and revised on a number of occasions. This will obviously mean that far more time will have to be devoted to budgeting processes over the whole of the financial year, but the extra costs involved should produce a system that will provide more effective controls in the battle for survival.

The sales budget is generally the first budget to be finalised as it is naturally extremely difficult to estimate business costs if information has not been provided regarding the expected level of activity. A few years ago it was possible to decide upon a selling price for the whole of the financial year and this was seldom varied. Today selling prices may change several times a year, although price legislation obviously limits company decision-making in this area. When there is so much uncertainty present in the system it is naturally extremely difficult to budget one year ahead, both from the point of view of quantity sales and estimated selling prices. In this situation, therefore, the policy recommended in the preceding paragraph may be the most appropriate, as detailed sales budget plans for a complete financial year may have to be scrapped or substantially revised after only a few months have passed.

In conditions of inflation there is naturally a great temptation to 'slash' those expenditure budgets which do not produce immediate returns for the business. In these circumstances budgets for personnel, training, research and some administrative costs have tended to suffer, although in the long term this rather negative type of policy can produce disastrous consequences. For the businessman who is fighting for survival this is an extremely difficult decision area. Perhaps the best advice that can be given is that no short-term decision should be made without considering the long-term consequences. When liquidation is threatening, however, it may be impossible to consider the long-term effects of any decisions that are made on the spur of the moment.

Capital Investment

Similar considerations frequently apply to capital investment decisions. At the present moment it is extremely difficult to estimate the benefits that will arise as a result of large capital expenditure projects, and recent surveys have suggested that many large companies are cutting back or abandoning capital investment plans. Once again this may be a short-sighted policy, but the businessman can hardly be blamed for such tactics if uncertainty and a very marked lack of confidence produce a situation in which it is virtually impossible to estimate the profits, if any, that will be made on capital projects. The advocates of more sophisticated methods of capital project assessment, for example, discounted cash-flow techniques, are therefore finding increasing resistance from the businessman who feels that it is almost impossible to project cash flows more than a year or so ahead. This is a most unfortunate situation because many large and medium-sized companies started to use discounted cash-flow systems in the 1960s, but now it seems that in many cases we are returning to a situation in which asset replacement decisions are frequently being left until it becomes virtually impossible to continue without acquiring new assets.

Cash Budgeting

Capital expenditure projects generally depend on the availability of cash resources, and it is therefore extremely important that the cash budget should be prepared as realistically as possible. In current conditions this budget should be constantly updated so that information is available regarding the times at which there will be severe shortages or large surpluses of cash. It is, of course, by no means certain that the projected deficit or surplus will materialise, but it is far better to have estimated figures than no figures at all. Action can be taken internally and externally in advance of anticipated cash shortages; for instance, an approach to a bank manager for higher overdraft facilities is far more likely to be successful if it is made several months in advance rather than at the last possible moment. Internal action could include amongst many possible alternatives a postponement of stock or fixed asset purchases, and rather different credit management policies.

Cash budgets may also be extremely useful in showing up the times of the year when surplus amounts of cash may be available. This will help in the timing of large expenditure projects, and it will also provide an opportunity for better cash utilisation; many local authorities, for example, offer very attractive interest rates for short-term investments. In the UK far too much money is kept in bank current accounts where it generally earns no interest; in addition, there will also be a loss in current conditions of approximately 2 per cent a month in purchasing power. In these circumstances bank current account balances should be kept to a minimum, and more use should be made of the bank deposit account. As far as the overdrawn current account is concerned cheques received should be banked as quickly as possible, and arrangements should be made for large cheques to be specially cleared. The reason behind this recommendation is that most banks do not take cheques received into account for interest purposes until three days after receipt. This is not appreciated by many businessmen who are operating with bank overdraft facilities.

Financial Performance

When the budget is finalised and the financial year commences it is most important that a close check be kept on actual financial performance, particularly as compared with budget figures. Departmental managers should be provided with regular financial information in readily understandable form as soon as possible after the end of each budget period. In most cases this will mean monthly reports, and these should include cumulative figures for the year as well as information for the relevant month. In current conditions accounting staff must give high priority to these reports, as delay may produce a situation in which there is very little that can be done about substantial variations from the original budget. A distinction should also be made, if possible, between controllable and non-controllable items so far as each departmental manager is concerned.

Ideally, budget figures should not become a straitjacket as such attitudes can produce extreme annoyance and frustration. On the other hand, too much flexibility can lead to a situation in which employees take little notice of the budget system. Management involvement is obviously essential since a 'tight' budget system may lead to many differences of opinion. Above all, it should be appreciated that there are many human problems involved in budgeting, and a careful reading of one or two of the recent books[3] on this subject could be of great help.

As time passes there will almost inevitably be some significant variations from the agreed budget. These variances may become extremely serious, and in certain circumstances it may be worthwhile drawing up a completely new budget, although this will, of course, be time-consuming. The old attitude that a budget should be drawn up only once a year and never be changed must now be questioned. This is especially true in the cash area, where daily revision may be essential today if the business is to survive.

Stock Control Systems and Credit Management Policies

The overall supervision of cash resources will generally involve very close scrutiny of stock control systems and credit management policies. The cost of holding stock in current conditions may well be in excess of 25 per cent per annum if all costs are taken into account—e.g. interest on funds used to purchase stock, space costs, supervision, insurance, theft, deterioration, etc. In these circumstances stock reductions can produce substantial savings, although sales and production managers will waste no time in stressing the dangers of low stockholding levels. In addition, the purchasing manager will almost inevitably point out how much can be saved by buying in large quantities before substantial price increases are effected. Once again this is an area where management involvement is generally essential in view of conflicting interests. Perhaps the most important point in current circumstances is that there should be a general awareness of the cost of holding stock. This does not mean that the end result will inevitably be a large reduction in stock levels as there are obviously significant costs involved in reordering and running out of stock.

It is also important that there should be a general awareness of the cost of granting credit. A few years ago generous credit terms were frequently used as a weapon in the battle for increased sales, but today this policy is extremely dangerous. Monthly information should be made available for management purposes, preferably in the form of an age analysis of debts outstanding. Insufficient attention has been paid to the quality of credit control staff in the past, but now it is slowly being appreciated that an efficient credit manager can save the firm many thousands of pounds. In 1974 it was taking UK manufacturing companies well over seventy days on average to collect outstanding debts. The efficient organisation should in most cases be able to improve on this, although inflation inevitably increases the advantage of delaying settlement. Many businessmen are now giving instructions for settlement to be delayed on the vast majority of accounts until the last possible moment. From the long-term point of view this may be a very damaging policy and could endanger supplies, but in the short term it may be one of several alternatives that will have to be considered in a financial crisis. The business that suffers in these circumstances is the one with a poor debtors control system. In current conditions, therefore, efficient debtors and creditors management is an essential part of any financial planning system.

Final Result

At the end of the financial year it might be suggested that the ideal result would be a net profit figure that corresponds with or exceeds the amount budgeted for in the financial planning system. With current uncertainties about the way in which profit should be measured there must inevitably be some reservations about this approach. Cash and working capital resources should also be examined in some detail, and comparisons made with the figures included in the budgeted balance sheet. Arguments will continue to rage for some time as to whether more attention should be devoted to profit figures or cash and working capital balances. At the present moment there is very little doubt that the liquidity position is the number one priority in many UK organisations, largely because of escalating costs. In the long term, however, only profits can generate adequate cash funds and there are obvious dangers in neglecting the level of net profit. Ideally, therefore, a financial planning system should consider all aspects of business performance, with particular emphasis on the level of profit and availability of cash resources. The latter area may have been somewhat neglected until comparatively recently, and in the long term the end result of our present difficulties may be far more efficient cash budgeting systems.

CONCLUSIONS

No organisation can survive as a result of past profit performance. Large retained profits in recent years may enable a firm to survive rather longer than would have been the case if all profits had been distributed, but in the vast majority of cases it will be future performance that will hold the key to success. This chapter has therefore been very much concerned with financial planning, although such a system is based in many respects on realistic records of past performance.

In current inflationary conditions there is little doubt that proper financial advice will be essential if many of our business organisations are to survive. It is not suggested, however, that the accountant has the cure for all our financial problems. Many accountants have a rather cautious and sometimes a negative attitude towards business problems, which may be damaging in normal conditions, but unfortunately we are not operating in normal circumstances at the present moment. In these rather unusual conditions it is hoped that this chapter will help to stimulate discussion amongst accountants and non-accountants regarding the financial policies that should be adopted under conditions of extreme inflation. If the policies suggested help a few business organisations to survive, the work involved in preparing this chapter will have been well worthwhile.

NOTES AND REFERENCES

1. This chapter was written before the publication of the Sandilands Committee report on inflation accounting. The Committee recommended a system that is very similar to the current replacement cost (CRC) accounting method mentioned earlier in this chapter. It is hoped to introduce this system for financial years commencing in December 1977.
2. For example, British Institute of Management, *Budgetary Control for the Smaller Company* (London, 1972); J. A. Scott, *Budgeting Control and Standard Costs*, Pitman (London, 1970); and A. H. Taylor and R. E. Palmer, *Financial Planning and Control*, Pan Books (London, 1969).
3. For example, G. H. Hofstede, *The Game of Budget Control*, Tavistock Publications, (London, 1968) and A. Hopwood, *Accounting and Human Behaviour*, Haymarket Publishing (London, 1974).

Index